"When you Go Deep, and God makes you into who He designed you to be, He will inevitably bring you to a calling to do something that is bigger than you."

-    David Bryant

GO DEEP

Discover All God
Created You to Be

by David Bryant

TRIBUTE PUBLISHING

2019

Tribute Publishing, LLC

Go Deep
First Edition March 2019

All Worldwide Rights Reserved
ISBN: 978-0-9998358-9-0

Printed in the United States of America

In God We Trust

In Loving Memory of

James Craig Williams

November 19, 1969 – May 18, 1990

Dedication

Go Deep is dedicated to the most important people in my universe, my family.

I am honored to be the father to Michael, Matt and Amanda. I could not be prouder of the men and woman you have grown to be. Bethany, Elise and Craig, you are gifts to our family. I am so very thankful that my sons and daughter found each of you. The greatest earthly blessings that could be given are the joys of our lives, Reagan, Madison, Landry and Harper. I am so proud to be their Pops. My prayer always is, you will see a glimpse of our heavenly father in me.

Over 40 years ago when I met LeeAnne, I knew she was out of my league. I hoped to meet someone like her because I never dreamed God would give her to me. I am forever thankful and overwhelmed that He did. Our journey together has had many turns and you have never wavered in going whatever direction life's road led us down, even when it didn't make sense. You are an incredible wife, mother and LaLa. Thank you for unconditionally believing in me and standing with me. You are a gift from God, and I will forever love and cherish you.

A Special Thanks to:

There are so many special people I have been blessed to share life with. I am humbled by those who have stood by me in both the good times and the difficult ones. The men mentioned below have dreamed with me, encouraged me when it would have been easier to give up, believed in me when I wasn't sure I believed in myself, and lifted my arms when I was weary. I am indebted to each of you and hope that I have been as good a friend to you as you have been to me.

Steve Yeary – Since we were teenagers, we have shared life. Even though miles have mostly separated us, our friendship and bond has remained strong, and for that, I am eternally grateful.

Dante Ramirez- God used your story to not only inspire this book but the calling for a movement of people to Go Deep and find all that God made each of us to be.
Thanks, D. for your friendship and support.

Dr. Bill Wright – I took a chance and did what writers aren't supposed to do and asked you to read the original manuscript. The Lord used you to validate what God was speaking to my heart. Thank you, my friend, your encouragement to me is more valuable than gold.

CONTENTS

"Let your roots grow down into Him,
and let your lives be built on Him."
Colossians 2:7 NLT

#godeepmovement

Chapter One

Introduction

Back in the day, there was a pretty simple grading system in school. A-C was passing, and D-F was failing. I will admit, I didn't live to go to school. I was the kid sitting in class looking out the window dreaming about baseball, the weekend, or whatever passed by at the moment. Even with that, I was a pretty consistent B-C student, depending on the subject. We won't talk about geometry, it didn't make sense then, doesn't make sense now, and I have yet to use it in over 40 years.

There was another grade worse than D-F, it was an I, meaning *incomplete*. I had a few of those on my school record when a project was never finished for whatever reason.

Like me, you have a few teachers from your school years that stand out to you. Mrs. Bigham was my eighth-grade social studies teacher. She was fiery and had a great passion for her students. One day there was an *incomplete* moment when I didn't finish an assignment. In front of the entire class, she says, "David Bryant, you are brilliant, but you will never accomplish anything in life unless you finish!" What she said was simple but powerful, so much so that I am telling you the story decades later. She was correct about the finishing part; I am not so sure about the brilliant comment.

I look back at my adult life, and I see *incompletes*, things started or just thought about, never brought to fruition. My guess is that all of us have at least one *incomplete* in our lives. In some cases, *incomplete* could be a positive if you started down a wrong road and something changed your course. But how about the good things that have been left unfinished?

Paul asked a powerful question to the church in Galatia,

"You were running a good race. Who cut in on you to keep you from obeying the truth?" (Galatians 5:7)

The church had started off well, with the right purpose, until false teaching crept in and moved the people away from the message of grace. We can ask ourselves the same question when we look back at our lives, who or what cut in?

In the eighteenth century, there was a tradition where women would pencil in names on a dance card. They would write the names of men they intended to dance with before they attended a formal ball. Movies have used the theme and storyline where the last name had been erased, and a new name was entered. Typically, it was a charming stranger who had cut in during a dance and won the heart of the lady. They would ride off into the sunset and live happily ever after, or not. At a single moment, unexpectedly, life and the future had changed. All because someone cut in.

It's in the changes of life our stories are written. Each of our lives is a book. Some of us have more chapters written than others. I am sure all of us have chapters we would rewrite if we could. If you are reading this, you still have chapters left to write and, like me, you have chapters to finish.

Philippians 1:6 says,

"He who began a good work in you will carry it on until completion, until the day of Christ Jesus."

Paul is speaking to believers whose lives had been changed, and their faith in Christ established. His purpose was to encourage them to keep growing and not stop like some in the church in Galatia.

The "things" that are incomplete in our lives are meaningless in comparison to our walk with the Lord, which is what Paul was referring to. As Christians, what we do should only be a product of what Jesus freely did for us on the cross. There is nothing we can do to earn what He did. The *incompletes* in our lives happen when something or someone cuts in on our faith.

In the chapters that follow, we will deal directly with the circumstances and situations that derail us during our journey and what we can do to get back to the place God has for us so we can finish. This book is about how we deepen our faith and understand that God is a God who completes all that He does.

Go Deep is about how we can take care of our *incompletes* and start new dreams. Sometimes, there is a dream hindered by one waiting to be completed. I don't know about your *incompletes*, but I certainly know about mine. The message here is not necessarily to go back and finish every assignment, but that it's never too late to change the grade of *incomplete*.

It is my prayer that my story and the chapters that follow will encourage and inspire others to know this. You will read stories that will refer to Scripture, which should be our only guide. I do not profess to be a theologian, you will not see any reference to what something means in Greek, but this book is intended to be authentic and relatable.

I believe there are many who have similar stories. There is a chance that I am like many of you, just a regular guy who wants to be better. Most of my life story has been written, and I realize the most important chapters are ahead. It is my passion to experience all that God has for me by finishing and leaving a legacy worth following.

Here is a little part of my story that I pray will connect with you as you join me on this journey to Go Deep.

MY STORY

My passion to Go Deep is the result of the journey I have been on for the past five years. It was following a time when my sisters and I had spent a decade caring for our parents as they struggled through the horrific disease of dementia. Every day across our country, adult children are faced with the reality of parenting their parents and making difficult decisions no one is truly prepared to make. After experiencing this difficult season in my life, I had arrived at a place of peace. I had some degree of contentment with my career and the direction I was headed professionally.

Chapter One – Introduction

Bob and Helen Bryant were good, hard-working people who succeeded at accomplishing almost 60 years of marriage. Our family was far from perfect, yet the greatest gift our parents gave us was a foundation of faith. Our lives always revolved around the local church. We moved many times due to my father's career and lived in Tennessee, Texas, Arkansas, and Missouri. In 1959, one of the moves landed my parents and two sisters in the East Texas town of Longview, where I was born. In my family, I have the proud distinction of being the only native Texan. We eventually settled in Dallas just before I entered the ninth grade.

The priority in all of the moves was to find a church home where we would attend all services. We would always get as involved as humanly possible. Such was the case in Dallas, and after a difficult first year of adjustment to the big city, my sister and I entrenched ourselves in our church. We built lifelong friendships, and in fact, to this day she is the longest serving staff member at the same church. For me, it was where I met my wife of 39 years, LeeAnne.

I was a shy, insecure kid, so I appreciated the friendships built in our church. My friends and I weren't declared saints; we just had good, mischievous fun. It was during my junior year in high school when I really tried to figure out what my purpose was. I got through school more because I had to than because it was my focus for the future.

Our church always provided a strong ministry emphasis mixed in with solid, fun activities. We were blessed with Youth Ministers and Pastors who poured the Word of God into our lives. They were strong examples, and because of their direction, I felt God tugging at my heart to serve in ministry. Honestly, to a shy, insecure kid, this created as much doubt as it did clarity. How could God use someone in ministry who was so uncomfortable being in front of people? Even with my doubts, I responded and made plans to attend Bible College in Springfield, Missouri.

The next 30 years consisted of marrying a wonderful, faithful woman, having three incredible kids, and a bi-vocational career mixed with ministry. Then I blew it all up. What followed was the most difficult years of my life. For the first time, everything I had believed in as a Christian became cloudy. I gave up my dreams and my identity. Slowly, God began to restore me. He never stopped loving me. I finally received His love and found peace with God, my family, and myself.

I found myself in the corporate business world where I believed I could be content and provide for my family. By this time, we had added two awesome daughters-in-law, a great son-in-law, and four absolutely perfect grandchildren. The problem was, God had created me for more. I found myself praying each day for God to fulfill His plan for me and to make me who He designed me to be. Trust me; it is a dangerous prayer.

Around the time of my father's passing in 2014, I told my wife I believed God was setting the stage for something. I wasn't sure what it was, but I knew God was preparing us for the most significant Kingdom days of our lives. It was then God began a work, a deep work, and a journey that continues to this day.

THE AUDIENCE

The question asked about most books is who the target audience is. When you explore the content, my hope is that it will spark interest within those who are hungry and fervent in their walk with the Lord; they just want more. If this is you, then I believe there is something for you in the pages ahead.

I believe it is also for the Christian who may be frustrated with trying to keep up with all the surface trappings of the world and in the church. For the one who is searching for answers and not sure what they are, please read on. I would be honored if you would take a chance to read the words written with an open heart. Finally, it is for all who have *incompletes* and the desire to change your grade and finish your story.

My earnest prayer is that God will use this book to move all who read it to know there is more. To know it is the plan of God to take each of us into the deep. Let's do it together, let's break through the surfaces of our lives, and let's Go Deep.

"Therefore, since we are surrounded by such a great cloud of witnesses, let us throw off everything that hinders and the sin that so easily entangles, and we run with perseverance the race marked for us, fixing our eyes on Jesus, the pioneer and perfecter of faith..."
(Hebrews 12:1-2)

Chapter One – Introduction

Chapter Two

First Things First

A friend of mine tells a story of asking his pre-teen daughters if he were to die, what words they would put on his tombstone? Their answer was, "cool dad." It made me wonder what my kids, who are now adults, would have said when they were the same age. Unfortunately, I have never had the distinction of being "cool" to my kids, whatever that means. Now, as I am nudging toward the age of 60 and my kids are married with their own families, I am sure the meaning has changed even more.

I am also keenly aware that the day is closer than I want to think when they will describe me as a memory. Now that my Dad is gone, my description of him is that he was a "good man." He was kind-hearted, hardworking, sensitive, jolly, loyal, and loved his family and friends. He was the farm boy from West Tennessee who left for the city, but his heart never left the fields and the work ethic instilled in him. It's not a bad way to be remembered, and I am blessed to have had a father who left me such a legacy.

If you have ever taken the time to look at what is engraved on memorials, you have caught a glimpse of how people felt about the person. There is one particular marker near my parent's grave that makes me smile when I walk by. It gives the pertinent information, and then the inscription says, "I told you I was sick!" Obviously, she was correct. Even though I would have said something different years ago, now I would be happy just to have one word describing me at my resting place: **Redeemed**. More than ever, I am thankful for the blood of Jesus shed on the cross for my sins. To think, it was God's purpose for His Son to take on the sins of the world so we could live free from the fear of death.

At the time of this writing, we have experienced the deaths of two prominent Americans in the past few months, Billy Graham, the greatest evangelist of our time and Barbara Bush, the beloved wife of our forty-first President and mother of the forty-third. Both lived long, distinguished lives into their 90's. Many stories were shared by the countless lives they had touched. Most telling were the words they shared as they prepared to enter heaven. Dr. Graham was quoted as saying, "Do I fear death? No, I look forward to death, with great anticipation. I am looking forward to seeing God face to face." After his death, the commentary was consistent, Billy Graham's message throughout his life was the same: the simplicity of the gospel of Jesus Christ and our need for a savior. Mrs. Bush was quoted as saying before her death, "I believe in Jesus, and He is my savior."

What confidence and peace in knowing that they had been redeemed and there was no fear of death. In fact, there was a great anticipation of being with Jesus.

LIFE TO THE FULL

Redemption is more than just assurance for when we die; it gives meaning to life here on earth.

Romans 14:9 states,

"For this very reason, Christ died and returned to life so that He might be the Lord of both the dead and the living."

Jesus himself said in John 10:10,

"I have come that they may have life and have it to the full."

Think about life to the full, not only the eternal life that is promised in John 3:16, but also life here on earth.

GRACE

The words you will read in the chapters ahead will not have meaning unless you understand the meaning of redemption and its product, grace. In the natural, it is impossible to understand grace and how to receive it. The reason is, I don't deserve it, none of us do. The natural response for all of us when we see the failure of humanity is to identify a person with their failure. Yet, as Christians, we should not operate in the realm of the natural, but in the spiritual due to our faith.

A lost world struggles to understand that the creator of the universe released mercy and grace upon sinful humanity through Jesus Christ. It is undeserved, yet He did it anyway; that is grace. For me, it was at six years old when I received that grace, obviously not a hardened criminal with a long history of failure. Even so, it was that moment at Vacation Bible School in Springfield, Missouri, where I understood my need for a savior. Then and many times throughout my life, I have come to a place of repentance, asking for mercy and grace I do not deserve. Yet, each time, He gives it.

It's not hard for Christians to look at a 6-year-old and accept the identity of a new believer. Unfortunately, it has become hard for many to grasp that grace also extends to the vilest of sinners, yet it does.

Romans 3:22-25 says,

"This righteousness is given through faith in Jesus Christ to all who believe. There is no difference between Jew and Gentile, for all have sinned and fall short of the glory of God, and all are justified freely by His grace through the redemption that came by Christ Jesus."

This passage speaks clearly that grace is not exclusive to a few, it is available to all, regardless of their origin or failure. To fully grasp what it means to Go Deep, you must understand God's gift of redemption and its product grace and its availability to all. Saul of Tarsus was one that some might feel was unredeemable. Yet the change in him after receiving Christ was so profound that he wrote much of the New Testament as the Apostle Paul. There is no difference today. God changes the hearts of men, women, boys, and girls, and makes them new, no matter their sin. It starts with this promise written by the same Paul.

"If you declare with your mouth, 'Jesus is Lord,' and
believe in your heart that God raised Him from the dead,
you will be saved." (Romans 10:9)

FRUIT

In 2016, the Barna group reported that three-quarters of Americans (73%) said they were Christian, while one-fifth (20%) claim no faith at all (that includes atheists and agnostics). A fraction (6%) identify with faiths like Islam, Buddhism, Judaism or Hinduism. One percent are unsure. Of the 73% professing to be Christians, only 31% attend church more than once a month. Do these numbers surprise you? Does America feel like the majority claim to have faith in Jesus Christ? Does our society reflect it? Do our churches?

There is great debate over whether church attendance is truly a reflection of the life of a Christian. There has been a dramatic change from my upbringing of mandatory attendance Sunday morning, Sunday night, and Wednesday night. So, let me kick off a thought that I am sure will raise some eyebrows. I don't believe church attendance is evidence of our walk with Christ. Instead, it is a byproduct of our walk with Christ. Evidence of our walk with Christ is living a redeemed life, which John called a "full life." A life that has been radically changed and transformed by confessing our sins, no matter how great or small, and receiving Jesus as our Savior.

Matthew 7 talks about more evidence of a redeemed life, fruit. Redemption is the theme of God's plan, and your story is part of that plan. My story is different from your story as far as the chapters, the plot, and the setting. What is the same is the theme, redemption. Our stories are given to us to share so that others will come to Christ and then our lives produce fruit.

"By their fruit will you recognize them." (Matthew 7:16)

WHERE IT ALL BEGAN

It was a brisk winter night when my wife and I met a group of neighbors at a popular barbeque restaurant in our town. The owner, Dante, is a close friend of mine who has his own wonderful redemptive story of how God has transformed his life. In a God-ordained moment, our paths had crossed and we quickly forged a friendship with common purposes in business and in our walks with Christ.

On this particular night, we were seated in what is called the VIP area which sits in front of the large barbeque pit, where Dante and his team work their magic. I sat and watched as my neighbors engaged in conversation while watching the pitmaster cut meat. This particular group of people had very diverse backgrounds, yet the conversation was rich and lively. The men were very interested in the art of smoking meat. Dante, always the consummate host, graciously gave us an education on what makes his product so special. I watched with fascination as my neighbors were enraptured with the demonstration.

It was then God began to speak to my heart with the vision to impact the Kingdom of God through the marketplace, by using the platforms and giftings He has given each of us. This led to the beginning of a marketplace movement called *Go Deep*. Dante's restaurant was the setting of the first conversation, where for six weeks a group of men were invited into a safe place where we sat at the same VIP table. It was an environment where we would hear Dante and others tell their stories.

We had conversations where we would challenge each other to be better men and not be satisfied with what was on the surface. It was non-judgmental; we were not trying to change people. When a person accepts Christ into their life and surrenders to Him, then the Holy Spirit works the change. It's His job, not ours. The work God does in someone's life is from the inside out, not the outside in.

When we Go Deep together, we love and accept each other and allow God to use our stories. It's then when individual discoveries can be made. The first group of men came from all walks of life. There were different ages, races, backgrounds, and each of us in a unique place in our relationship with the Lord. We were different, yet around the table we were the same.

THE FORMULA

In Psalm 107, the Psalmist laid out the formula for Go Deep. The chapter begins with thanksgiving, when it says,

"Give thanks to the Lord, for He is good, His love endures forever." (Psalm 107:1)

This verse is critical because it sets the tone for the message of redemption and the power of God's love. Verse 2 gives direction when it says,

"Let the redeemed of the Lord share their story."

Verses 4-6 describe those who were homeless and hungry and then they,

"Cried out to the Lord in their trouble and He delivered them from their distress."

Verses 10-13 talks about those in darkness and in bondage because of their rebellion, and they also,

"Cried to the Lord in their trouble and He saved them from their distress."

Verses 17-20 speaks to those who are sick and dying because of their rebellious ways. Then they, too,

"Cried to the Lord in their trouble and He saved them from their distress."

The fourth group described in verses 23-24 are the merchants of the sea. The Scripture talks about how,

"They saw the works of the Lord, His wonderful deeds in the deep."

You will see reference to these words throughout the book. We will discover what they saw in the deep and what God has for each of us. These rugged men of the sea experienced the wonders of God through the highs and lows of their journey. They, too,

"Cried out to the Lord in their trouble, and He brought
them out of their distress." (Psalm 107:28)

In all four scenarios, God showed up in their stories
and they gave thanks for what the New International Version
calls the Lord's "unfailing love." 32 times, mostly in Psalms,
we see this description. Other translations call it steadfast
love, great love, his goodness, faithful love, and loving
kindness. No matter the interpretation, it speaks of the
power of God's love for us.

This love is the basis for our redemption spoken
plainly in John 3:16,

"For God so LOVED the world that He GAVE His one
and only SON, that whoever believes in Him shall not
perish but have eternal life."

For me, it wasn't until my first son was born, did I
realize the magnitude of the Father's love. No matter how
much I loved someone, there is no way I would have given
my son up for them. It was inconceivable, yet God did it, for
you and for me. I have failed God more times than I want to
think about and still, His love is so perfect and so unfailing,
that it covers me.

I have a picture on the wall of my office. It's the first
thing I see each morning. It says,

"Let the morning bring me word of Your unfailing love, for
I have put my trust in You. Show me the way I should go,
for to You I entrust my life." (Psalm 143:8)

17

It reminds me that no matter what happened the previous day, no matter how I failed, each morning is new, and His love does not fail and cannot fail.

"Because of the Lord's great love, we are not consumed, for His compassions never fail. They are new every morning; great is Your faithfulness."
(Lamentations 3:22-23)

It doesn't give me a license to sin or to live in defeat, just the opposite, redemption gives me the ability to live life to the full. (Romans 6:1-2)

What about you? Are you fully alive? Have you been redeemed? Do you not fear death because of the promise of eternal life? If so, what is your story and who have you told? Someone in your life needs to hear it, and only you can tell it. You don't have to stand in a pulpit or be a pastor. Jesus uses the fishermen, the plumber, the ball player, the accountant, and the restaurant owner. Your story will bring them hope and to Christ.

You can have knowledge of God and know the Bible backward and forwards, but without a personal relationship with Jesus Christ, then you are not fully alive. It is critical to understand, to Go Deep is not only about gaining more knowledge, but it's also about deepening your relationship with our personal God. Paul said it powerfully in Philippians 3:10,

"I want to know Christ-yes, to know the power of His resurrection and participation in His sufferings, becoming like Him in His death."

The first step is always to receive Christ and be redeemed. Many stop there and fail to understand there is more. We must know Him, and the more we know Him, the more we become like Him. It doesn't matter how much you have accomplished on the surface or how much you have failed. The offer is the same. He offers each of us the gift of redemption and the opportunity to know Him.

If you haven't taken the first step, it's not too late. In fact, it's time. Call out to Him in whatever place you are, and He will hear you and respond. If you have received Him, know there is more, and it is God's desire to take you to a deeper place in Him. Are you ready? If so, Jesus is ready to write your story.

Chapter Two – First Things First

Chapter Three
Spindletop Hill

The story of Spindletop Hill is a fascinating one. It is a major piece of the history of Texas oil production. We Texans are a proud group, and some of us continue to brag about our independence. Much of that is due to the rich heritage of the oil industry.

Spindletop is located in Beaumont, which is in the far southeast corner of the state near the Louisiana border. Oil in Texas dates back to the Native Americans. At this time in the 1800s, oil was mostly produced from the surface where there was known seepage. The production met the need of the day even though there were suspicions there could be oil underground.

Pattillo Higgins was an early entrepreneur who had a variety of business interests, including being a self-taught geologist. He was one who believed there were greater riches to be found beneath the surface. The difference was that he was willing to do something about it. He was not satisfied with the status quo and determined to discover all the earth had to give.

Higgin's had to overcome many obstacles in his personal life that led him to Spindletop Hill. He was not going to let a physical handicap or mistakes made in his youth keep him from making a difference in his world.

NEVER SATISFIED

As I have studied the life of Pattillo Higgins, I have found him fascinating. Here is a man who could have gone to prison, or even ended up dead. He could have settled or felt limited due to his circumstances. Instead, he let nothing stop him from taking risks and taking hold of everything life had for him. He truly was a man who was not going to be satisfied with living on the surface.

I had never heard of the history of Spindletop or of Higgins until God began to move in my heart to launch Go Deep. I am drawn to stories like this and to risk-takers who aren't satisfied. My life has been laced with segments when I have ventured off the path to find what else lay undiscovered. For a long time, I considered it a weakness because I wasn't one of those guys who could lock into the same job for decades. I now believe it is who God made me to be, sometimes much to the chagrin of my loyal and faithful wife.

LeeAnne was raised in a great family; her father was a successful high school coach and athletic director who stayed in the same job for many years. Fortunately for me, God knew exactly who I needed to keep me balanced. She is also the one who may not always understand my different mindset, but she always supports and believes in my latest cause.

Those who choose to Go Deep, do so because they aren't satisfied. Like Pattillo Higgins, they believe there is more beneath the surface.

LIVING ON THE SURFACE

I have taught my kids that the things that are of the greatest value in life are not easy; they take work and effort. Our culture has created things to be simpler, easier, and take less effort, often referred to as a "microwave society." It's not necessarily bad until it becomes a mindset and lifestyle. I fear for a generation that has found things too easy and have become satisfied. Even worse, when they aren't easy, they give up and quit. The tragedy of marriage is that because they weren't as easy as believed they should be, couples give up and refuse to fight for its value. Today, we see a generation that has watched many marriages fail. Therefore, many have decided they don't need it and opt out.

There is a prevailing mindset in our society today. We are satisfied with surface living, what we can see, and what the world sees. We gauge success by how much money someone has or what possessions they own.

After raising our kids in the suburbs of Dallas, we experienced this mindset firsthand. We built a new house in a new development a few years ago. It has been a frustrating and fantastic experience. If you have ever built a house, you understand what I mean. We have a great community of new neighbors, all in new homes. Most of us moved out of the city to gain more space, less traffic, and the quiet of the country.

Once in a new home, it's fun to watch all the additions begin, things like pools, landscaping, and additional buildings. I see someone add something and it gets my wheels churning to follow suit. There is absolutely nothing wrong with this unless it becomes our purpose and forms our identity. The fact is, it's all surface and its value is temporary.

Churches can do the same with new buildings and the belief they will attract more people. The danger is if the real reason the church exists begins to be watered down, it will lose its purpose.

PENDULUM SWING

Does it seem like in some ways, today's church is suffering from an identity crisis? The pendulum has swung away from tradition, and many have found themselves trying to appeal to pop culture. Some believe by changing their name and style, it will attract non-believers and bring people back to church.

I am not a traditionalist, nor do I consider myself a legalist. I was raised in a very strict Christian home where it seemed like nothing was OK. Many of my generation rebelled against that bondage and ran from the church. This is one reason why generations today seemingly have no sense of who God really is. I am thankful that I didn't run from the church and realized that God's laws and man's laws are not always the same. The freedom He gives through Jesus is actually liberating.

I am not looking for a return to the old-time religion of my upbringing. I personally am a business casual kind of guy and enjoy that atmosphere. I also believe God uses the technology available today. In fact, He has gifted a generation to create some of the most amazing things. What must be engrained in us, though, is that we cannot be satisfied and depend on the "things" God has created to reach people, we must always rely on the creator of the "things." It's not our job as Christians to be concerned with keeping up with what the world offers, because it is surface.

My comments have nothing to do with old worship songs vs. new worship songs; I love them all. What it does mean is believing and depending on the Word of God and its power to change people's lives, not the latest fad. If God is our focus, then it doesn't matter what the building looks like or what we wear because our eyes are firmly on Jesus.

The surface things of life can be marriages without a solid foundation, houses and possessions, and churches overly focused on appealing to pop culture. None of these will meet the deep spiritual need of our hearts. The world is looking for authenticity and the place they should find it is in God's people, who are not perfect but should be real.

Remember my comment in the last chapter about God working through people from the inside out, not outside in? In the same vein, the church was not built from the inside out but the outside in. The followers of Jesus ministered in the marketplace and lives were transformed, and hence, the church was formed. Building from the outside in doesn't mean we stop doing mission trips and outreach ministries, it just means building disciples should be the highest calling of the church, to equip people to use their personal platforms to tell their story to a world that desperately needs to hear it.

Doing life on the surface may bring temporary satisfaction, but the only thing that can truly satisfy the needs of our souls is Jesus. (John 4:13-14) He is not a fad or a trend, He is the same yesterday, today and forever. (Hebrews 13:8)

FAILURE

The story of Spindletop also includes failure. There were many attempts that came up dry and caused investors to run away from the venture. The fear of failure can be paralyzing. We live in a society that expects instant success and is not tolerant of mistakes or failures.

In Dallas, a sport-driven city, the fan base is impatient when the teams come up short. We aren't satisfied with just making the playoffs or having a winning season; we demand championships. Unfortunately, we have been dissatisfied for many years now.

The truth is, success typically comes after failure. Seven times Abraham Lincoln was defeated while running for either office or nomination. Before the Wright brothers ever flew a plane, their story was laced with failure, but they persisted. When we think of Lincoln, it's as of one of our greatest Presidents, and when we think of the Wright Brothers, it is for their success in creating flight, not about their failures. What drove Lincoln to continue running for office and the Wright brothers to pursue flying when clearly their track records weren't in their favor?

The difference in those who Go Deep is how they respond to their failure. Truth be known, we have all failed at something in our lives, but how many have quit and never tried again? Those who don't quit are driven by the passion to change the world and the belief that there is more: a better life and a better person. It's easy not to try and it's easy to quit.

It took many attempts at Spindletop before they hit a gusher. What was it about Pattillo Higgins that made him refuse to quit? Was it because he had a story and his story made him stronger, more persistent, and more passionate to change the world? I believe his past and the memories of how far he had come drove him. He knew he had changed because of the deep work that had happened in his life.

Do you have a dream that drives you and won't allow you to sleep at night? Is it a dream that is bigger than you and consumes you? If so, then the world needs your dream. More than likely you will stumble along the way, but just make sure you get back up and continue to move forward. Let your failure drive you even harder, and if everyone around you leaves you, God will never leave you. (Deuteronomy 31:8)

The secret which shouldn't be a secret is what happened to Pattillo Higgins. When Jesus came into his life and did a deep work, it changed him, and his failures didn't matter. Because he was changed, he then changed his world.

RISK

The story of Spindletop is about going deep to find the unknown. Make no mistake, it would have been easiest just to continue to produce from above ground. It was sure and proven, but nothing of value is ever easy. Dr. Tony Evans, a hero of the faith, says, "If you want a diamond you have to dig for some coal. God's got all his valuable stuff underneath the ground." Will you take the risk, pay the price, and not be satisfied? Are you willing to overcome every obstacle and find all that God has for you? Going beneath the surface is about the passion to discover what the Psalmist meant with the description, "His wonderful deeds in the deep."

The first challenge Pattillo Higgins had was to convince others that it was worth the risk to drill. To do so would require more time, more money, and more effort. He had to overcome the mindset of those who were satisfied. Why take the risk if it wasn't necessary? It would be different if there was a lack of oil, but that wasn't the case. They knew what they had always done was giving them what they always had. So why change? Why take the risk? And what if they failed?

PHILLY SPECIAL

As tough as it is for a lifelong Cowboys fan to admit, in my opinion, the greatest play in Super Bowl history was made by our arch rivals, the Philadelphia Eagles, in Super Bowl LII. The storyline was incredible. The Eagles star quarterback had been sidelined before the playoffs began, and the team had been written off. They were led by Nick Foles, a journeyman, who had played for several teams. Foles lived up to the challenge and led his team to the big game. Still, no one expected them to win.

It was the second quarter and the Eagles were leading the New England Patriots 15-12 as the first half was coming to an end. The 5-time champion Patriots are coached by Bill

Belichick and led by arguably the best quarterback in the history of the NFL, Tom Brady.

The Eagles had the ball on the Patriots' one-and-a-half-yard line on fourth down. The usual and seemingly safe decision would be to kick a field goal and expand the lead going into halftime. Second-year coach Doug Pederson decided differently. He knew that most of America expected Brady to rally his team as he had the year before against the Atlanta Falcons. He realized the city of Philadelphia had long waited for this moment and he could not let them down, so he went for it. What did they have to lose? No one expected his team to win anyway.

The center sent a direct snap back to the running back, who then tossed the ball to the wide receiver, Trey Burton. He then threw a simple pass in the end zone to the wide open Foles for a touchdown.

The message it sent to both teams as they entered the locker rooms was momentous. There was no comeback this year and the Philadelphia Eagles became the World Champions for the first time in their history. It's impossible to know if Brady had a comeback in his pocket. I believe when Coach Pederson decided to take an incredible risk against conventional wisdom, the game was then won.

Even as a Cowboys fan, I have immense respect for Pederson and his players. To me, it is not a coincidence that he, Foles, and their injured quarterback, Carson Wentz, are committed Christ followers. They openly shared their faith before and after the game. I believe it was that faith, instilled in their hearts, that gave them the courage to take the risk.

No one changes their world without doing something that hasn't been done before. Many times, it means going against conventional wisdom and the voices of the crowd. When Doug Pederson had his team line up to run another play, the "experts" were saying, "What is he doing?" When Pattillo Higgins decided to drill underground, the naysayers were telling him he had lost his mind. Both did it anyway, and as a result, you are reading about them today, not because they failed, but because they tried. They took the risk.

When you make the decision to Go Deep in your life, it will mean doing something different from what the world prescribes. Trust me, there will be naysayers and doubters, there always are. Some will want to remind you of your failures because it reminds them of theirs. You may be abandoned and feel alone. However, the reward will be a full life, things that you can't even imagine, but first, you have to decide to take the risk.

Allow the story of Spindletop Hill and Pattillo Higgins to inspire you to move to a place that may not be comfortable. It may be a place that you left behind because of failure or disappointment. It's never too late to start over, to Go Deep, and discover all God has for you.

Chapter Four
Texas Clay

My two-year-old grandson, Landry, is all boy. His passion is rocks and anything with four wheels. It doesn't matter whether it is a car or a truck, he is fascinated by it. Everywhere he goes, he has a collection with him and he is fiercely protective of them. Like most boys, I had a hot wheel's track as a kid, but Landry takes it to a whole new level. He checks under the hood and knows every part and what it does. Did I tell you he is an amazing kid? To be clear, he didn't get his passion for cars from our side of the family. I like to drive a nice car or truck, but to me, the only way to fix one is to find the best mechanic. Then there is his other grandfather who is a car dealer and restorer. Bob will find an old car or truck in remote places, normally not running, and get it to his garage where he works miracles. My prediction is that Landry will either follow his other grandfather's footsteps, or he will become the next Dale Earnhardt Jr.

Not long ago, we were taking Landry and his sister Reagan home and out of the blue he shouts, "EXCAVATOR!" Did I tell you this kid is amazing? This particular excavator was taking out a pretty good-sized hill on a major road in our town. There had been a building on top of the hill that had been demolished, and now they were removing the hill to street level to build a new, bigger building. I drove this route on a daily basis and was amazed to see the disciplined daily progress of the excavator as it dug through the dirt and within a short amount of time, there was no longer a hill.

To dig through any amount of dirt in North Texas is no small feat. In fact, we don't call it dirt, it's clay. Digging into clay is some of the most difficult work when preparing for a building. I have had people from other parts of the country ask me why we don't have many basements in our homes. It's not impossible, but the digging is difficult and there is a chance of the ground cracking during dry, hot times of the year. This causes a high percentage of foundation problems, which has created an industry with many "specialists" that want to put lifts under our houses to make them level again. Having had this done once to a previous home, it is not an inexpensive process.

DIGGERS

It makes sense that excavators are also called "diggers." It is the first to break through the hard, clay surface. It's hydraulic and has a bucket attached to a dipper or stick controlled by the operator in a cab on a rotating platform. They come in all sizes and are used based on the depth of the project. The deeper they go, the more excavators are used, and the higher the eventual structure will be.

When we decide to Go Deep in our lives, the first and possibly hardest task is breaking ground. Just like the hard Texas clay giving resistance to a new building, the surface of our lives will do the same. Let me be clear, God is a powerful God who is capable of flooding the earth during the time of Noah, parting the Red Sea for Moses and the children of Israel, and raising His Son from the dead to give us life, but God does not force His way in. He gives us the power to choose. Jesus said,

"Here I am! I stand at the door and knock. If anyone hears My voice and opens the door, I will come in and eat with that person, and they with Me." (Rev 3:20)

He doesn't break the door down, He knocks and offers us the chance to open the door. Sadly, many have refused to allow Him in. If we really understood the magnitude of that decision, I can't imagine our choice would be the same. Unfortunately, we get caught in the surface trappings of our lives, and it clouds the truth and promises of God's Word.

THE TRUTH

Recently, I had a friend pull me aside at a family gathering. He is not a believer and he asked me if we could get together and talk about what happens when we die. Like most in their mid-60's, I could tell the thought of his mortality was on his mind. As we talked, he went on to say he had visited with ministers and even a rabbi to hear what they had to say. Sadly, he had walked away from those conversations and made the decision that there was nothing after this life, that when we die, we just become part of the dirt. He is a good man who I care about, and as I listened, my heart was moved and honestly somewhat optimistic because he was asking questions. To me, it meant his surface was a little softer. I don't know if I was able to alter his decision as I talked to him about the choice God gives us to believe because He loves us. I saw in his eyes the sincere desire to know the truth. I didn't sense pride or arrogance, just a man seeking answers.

My friend is not alone; I truly believe we live in a world with masses of people seeking the truth and wanting what is real. They are grabbing hold of every new fad our culture has to offer to find the fulfillment that believers know only comes through knowing Jesus. I will not give up on my friend, I will keep asking God to reveal Himself, and I will continue to love him and be there to talk with him whenever he needs.

GIVE US A KING

One of the most tragic stories in the Bible is of a man who missed his destiny. It is the story of the first King of Israel. God had delivered the children of Israel from the Egyptians, and whenever times would get tough, they would turn their back on God and worship other gods.

Samuel, the prophet, was old and the Israelites were concerned that they would not have a leader when he died, so they asked him to appoint a King. It's interesting, the reason they wanted a King was because other nations had one. (1 Samuel 8:5) God's chosen people were asking to be like everyone else, no longer set apart. Once again, they had lost their dependence on the one true God.

The Lord spoke to Samuel and said,

"Listen to all that the people are saying to you, it is not you they have rejected, but they have rejected Me as their king." (1 Samuel 8:7)

Today, we continue to see people looking for earthly kings to follow and serve, rejecting the only one who can truly satisfy the longing of our souls.

Reluctantly, Samuel, obeying God, granted their request and gave them a Benjamite named Saul. He had all the physical attributes that people look for in a leader. He was tall and handsome. He was humble, and because he was from the smallest tribe, he felt unqualified to be King. Let's never forget God's qualification starts with humility. It is a heart that is surrendered to God that He anoints and uses.

After Samuel anointed Saul by pouring oil from a flask, he set out to follow God's plan. Samuel said to Saul,

"The Spirit of the Lord will come powerfully upon you, and you will prophesy with them; and you will be changed into a different person." (1 Samuel 10:6)

The Scripture goes on to say in verse 9 that,

"God changed Saul's heart."

He was God's man to lead His people. What an incredible honor to be the first King of Israel. Samuel then declared to the Israelites,

"There is no one like him among all the people."
(1 Samuel 10:24)

The Israelites had sinned against God time and time again by worshipping other gods. The appointment of a King was a product of their rebellion even though it was not the plan of God. They were given a chance to repent. As Samuel prepared them for his departure, he declared,

"If you fear the Lord and serve and obey Him and do not rebel against His commands, and if both you and the king who reigns over you follow the Lord your God - good!"

Wait for it...

"But if you do not obey the Lord, and if you rebel against His commands, His hand will be against you, as it was against your ancestors." (1 Samuel 12:14-15)

Saul and the people had a chance; God granted them grace to start fresh, to move forward with another chance, all they had to do was Go Deep and serve only the one true God.

It didn't take long before Saul began to show his greatest weakness, the sin of self-dependence. When God didn't act on Saul's timing, Saul would act on his own. He did not obey Samuel's instructions to the point where the Lord said,

"I regret that I have made Saul king because he has turned away from Me and has not carried out My instructions."
(1 Samuel 15:10)

What a tragic situation to have God regret that He has chosen you. Even though Saul reigned over Israel for 42 years, his tenure was tragic. He continued to spiral out of control and greed, dishonesty, jealousy, and the desire to please men over God became his main focus.

Fast forward to Samuel going to Jesse's sons and choosing the least, the shepherd boy David to be the eventual King of Israel. There is much to read about the relationship between Saul and David. The more that God would raise up David, the more insecure Saul would become. Saul eventually committed suicide and his tragic life would end.

Think about the reigns of Saul and David. God was forceful in His rebuke of Saul for his rebellion to the point of rejecting him as King. David also failed God in perhaps a far greater way than Saul. Why didn't God reject David in the same way? The difference was David's heart. He was a man after God's own heart and from an early age had God's touch on his life. David's sins were great as was his brokenness and repentance. He owned up to his failure and humbled himself before the Lord. He went deep into his heart and cried out to God in Psalm 51:1,

"Have mercy on me, O God according to Your unfailing love;..."

He acknowledged the greatness of God. He repented of his sin and asked to be cleansed in v.2 and v.7. He asked the Lord for a pure heart, and a renewed, steadfast spirit in v.10. He committed to the Lord that he would use his story to bring sinners back in v.13.

Psalm 51 is the key to breaking the surface of our hearts in order to allow the Lord to Go Deep. The hard clay can be excavated with the power of brokenness. None of us need to follow in the footsteps of Saul no matter how hard the surface of our hearts may be. In some ways, it's easier to be broken after failure than it is when things are going well in our lives. The danger is when pride and self-sufficiency take over, then there is no ability or desire to break the surface. Inevitably though, it catches up with all of us and Proverbs 16:18 says,

"Pride goes before destruction, a haughty spirit before a fall."

BREAKTHROUGH

We do not need to fail in order to humble ourselves before the Lord. I am sure if all of us could go back and make different decisions throughout our lives we would, but we can't. We do have the journey forward. My passion is that of Paul, to fight the good fight, to finish the race and to keep the faith.

On the North Dallas Tollway, there is a huge hole that appeared in the middle of a vacant field. It was the work of many excavators that would make my grandson Landry very happy as they dug into the Texas clay. Once they had broken through the surface, the equipment began to disappear. It was still there, but it was now underground doing its work unseen. Sometimes it begins with land that has always been bare and sometimes it is where a structure once stood. It could have been destroyed, or it could have become deserted and rotted away. No matter the cause, it is now time to move forward and build something even greater than before.

Experts tell me that the deeper they dig and the more work they do beneath the surface, the greater the new structure will be when it rises. The same is true as we Go Deep and allow the Holy Spirit to work in our lives. The deeper the work, the greater the significance of what God does through our lives. The step here in going deep is to humble ourselves as David did. It's more than just deciding you want more, it's surrendering your pride and self-sufficiency to allow the breakthrough. That tough, Texas clay represents our stubborn will resisting the excavator. The excavator is the Holy Spirit, breaking through to discover the "wonderful deeds in the deep."

"If my people, who are called by my name, will humble themselves and pray and seek my face and turn from their wicked ways, then I will hear from heaven, and I will forgive their sin and will heal their land."
(2 Chronicles 7:14)

Chapter Four – Texas Clay

Chapter Five
The Dump

Have you ever been to a garbage dump? Most municipalities have a location away from the city limits that serve as a place for residents to get rid of junk. Officially the word is landfill, in reality, it is a graveyard for all the things in our lives we no longer have a use for.

There are actually excavators in these dumps that are constantly digging and covering up the endless amounts of garbage. They bury it, cover it up and bury more until that landfill is at capacity, then it's on to a new location.

When you Go Deep beneath the surface of your life, more than likely you are going to find your own personal landfill. It could be a hidden sin that you do not want to expose, a broken relationship, or a memory of a painful time in your life. Let's face it, this journey called life does include pain and suffering.

THE MYTH

One of the biggest myths of Christianity is that Christians have perfect marriages, perfect kids, never lose their jobs or struggle with money. It's a false narrative that we just tiptoe through the tulips until we go to be with Jesus. Many new believers have lost their way due to the fact that life didn't become easier than it was before they found their faith in Christ.

The first chapter of James dispels this myth when he says,

"Consider it pure joy, my brothers and sisters, whenever you face trials of many kinds because the testing of your faith produces perseverance. Let perseverance finish its work so that you may be mature and complete, not lacking anything." (v.2-5)

This Scripture has been a mainstay for me personally, and I have shared it many times with friends facing a challenge. It's hard to get past the "consider it pure joy" start to the passage. I can't honestly tell you that I get excited when facing a trial. It's those times in life when you don't have an answer and the pain feels unbearable that James is speaking of. It's a big picture verse that gives us promise that through the pain, there is purpose, and that purpose is to make us "complete, not lacking anything."

This passage gives hope to Christians who embrace it to know that it is God's desire to be continually working in our lives through both the good times and the hard times. When we are in the midst of the trial, we find ourselves open to God because of our need. Without the trial, our human nature is to turn less to God and be more self-sufficient. God uses our brokenness for His glory. The question is, what impact does the trial have for you long term?

Like so many Scriptures we embrace, the reading is the easy part; it's the applying to our life that takes work. Unfortunately, all of us have failed to allow God's process to work and we either take matters into our own hands or give up too soon. It's then the struggle becomes real, and without trusting God, we then turn to the surface things to find a solution.

God gives us the formula to be whole, yet He gives us a choice to receive and obey His Word. When we fail to follow the plan of God, then the garbage begins to build up and poisons our thought processes and controls our lives. We take things into our own hands because we are impatient or because the solution we want doesn't line up with God's will. We then create more garbage.

GARBAGE IN - GARBAGE OUT

In the early days of technology, there was a phrase used by programmers: garbage in and garbage out. What was loaded into a system, produced what came out. If you put in good information then you receive good data, bad information gave you bad data.

We have the daily opportunity to allow things into our lives that will either build us up or tear us down. When we choose to live by the principles of God's Word, then we produce Godly fruit, and when we don't, we must live with the consequence. This is the principle of sowing and reaping talked about in Galatians 6:7-8,

"A man reaps what he sows. Whoever sows to please their flesh, from the flesh will reap destruction; whoever sows to please the Spirit, from the Spirit will reap eternal life."

Verse 9 then says,

"Let us not become weary in doing good, for at the proper time we will reap a harvest if we do not give up."

Think back to James when God talks about the process to make us complete, then Galatians talks about not giving up when we get tired of waiting. Make no mistake about it, God is deliberate in His timing. The more difficult the test, the more significant the work is that God wants to do. Too often we fail that test and create much of the pain that produces more garbage.

FEAR

The driving factor is the same issue we talked about in the story of Spindletop Hill: fear. We fear change and we fear losing the kingdoms we have built. Let's be clear, fear of anything but God is not from God and reaps confusion and causes people to turn their back on anything to do with God. Paul very plainly says to Timothy,

"For the Spirit God gave us does not make us timid (fear), but gives us power, love, and self-discipline."
(2 Timothy 1:7)

Fear is an emotion, not a tangible substance. It is the product of a thought that we allow to enter our mind. It then camps out under the surface and begins to do its own damage and will create more thoughts that then lead to action or behavior. There are many things that become garbage in our lives, but I believe fear is many times the ignitor. Fear of rejection, fear of loss, fear of failure, fear of the future, or fear of death are a few.

Fear must be dealt with, and it starts when the thought enters our mind. 2 Corinthians 10:5 says,

"We demolish arguments and every pretension that sets itself up against the knowledge of God, and we take captive every thought to make it obedient to Christ."

Recognize the power in this verse is given to you and me. "WE demolish," "WE take captive," it is in our control. We must face the fear and recognize where it comes from and then stand on the word of God to deal with it.

Fear paralyzes.
Steals hope.
Extinguishes faith.
Derails the future.

Perfect love drives out fear.
1 John 4:18

Paul also said in His admonition to Timothy that the Spirit of God gives us self-discipline. It is a God-given ability to calmly recognize a thought when it comes into our mind and immediately take it captive. Did you know that self-discipline is a gift from God? He did not make us weak, mindless robots who just sway in the wind until He moves. He gives us the things we need to take action as we step out in faith and courage.

Three times, God told Joshua to be "strong and courageous" after the death of Moses as He prepared the children of Israel to move into the promised land (Joshua 1). The opposite of fear is courage and it is a command of God when facing the challenges of life.

THE UNEXPECTED

Several years ago, I faced an unexpected job change; I was a victim of corporate downsizing, a situation many in the business world deal with on a far too regular basis. This was new to me, and even though it wasn't a job I was passionate about it, it certainly brought its share of concern to my wife and me. All the things we counted as earthly security had been taken from us. I was in my mid 50's, not the ideal candidate, and honestly didn't have an answer as to which direction I should go to take care of my family.

What I now know was that it was a part of the journey in the deep. God was calling me to be courageous and steadfast in trusting Him. I focused very intently on His Word. It was critical to feed my mind with Scripture to find courage. I listened to many sermons from men like Dr. Evans who opened the Word to me and spoke truth into my life. Nightly I would wake with the words of Kari Jobe's song, "I am Not Alone" playing in my mind. The lyrics are simple and powerful. It was the way God knew how to speak deep into my spirit. As a teenager, I would lay in bed at night, listening to the music of the day as I contemplated life. Understand, the lyrics to Kari's song are more than creative words. The key theme is based out of Deuteronomy 31:8 when Moses challenged Joshua as he passed the torch,

"The Lord himself goes before you and will be with you; He will never leave you nor forsake you. Do not be afraid; do not be discouraged."

I look back at those months as a marker where God proved Himself faithful to us because we remained obedient to His Word and trusted Him. I went back to the same company in another position for a few more years until I felt led to leave to continue on the journey we are on now. What happened then prepared me for today as we have stepped out in faith to fulfill God's calling for our lives.

I have not always handled challenges in life like that. In fact, more times than not, the story has been different and instead of feeding the Word of God into my life, I would look for surface solutions. The result would typically create bitterness, un-forgiveness, and insecurity, which are my personal weaknesses that created garbage. For some, the weakness can be turning to alcohol, drugs, or a wrong relationship that fills the landfill. Whatever the weakness, when it gains control, it forms a wound within your soul.

OPEN WOUNDS

Our society is full of wounded people. It has become the norm to mask wounds with outward appearance, yet deep inside many people are broken. It may be from a family situation, a job loss, a health issue or a multitude of other reasons. No matter the cause, we know that we serve a God who cares and who is with us.

Psalm 34:18 says,

"The Lord is close to the brokenhearted and saves those who are crushed in spirit."

Psalm 147:3 promises,

"He heals the brokenhearted and binds up their wounds."

Personally, I have many scars, and I am OK with that. Scars are reminders of wounds that have healed. They may be unsightly, but they serve a purpose. The danger is when we don't allow the wound to heal and it continues to ooze garbage into our lives. Sometimes, we purposely keep the wound from healing because we can't let go of whatever happened in the past. A wound can become bigger or create another wound, and even more garbage comes out of our lives. Typically, when the garbage reveals itself, it comes out against others and more lives are impacted.

It doesn't have to be garbage in, garbage out. Because of the scars that Jesus bore, the wounds can be healed.

"He was pierced for our transgressions, He was crushed for our iniquities; the punishment that brought us peace was on Him, and by His wounds, we are healed."
(Isaiah 53:5)

The first step to be healed emotionally and spiritually, is to recognize the wounds in our soul and take responsibility. It is then that the garbage in our lives can be removed. It only happens because of the gift that Jesus gave each of us on the cross. It doesn't mean garbage won't continue to form, it will. The key is a daily surrender and the willingness to allow God to go deep in our lives.

GOD HELP US

As I work on this chapter, today becomes another day that has become far too common in our country. A 17-year-old opened fire on his school in Santa Fe, Texas, killing ten people. It was just February earlier the same year that a 19-year-old killed 17 in a Parkland, Florida high school. This will further ignite the political debate over gun control and how we can become defenders to protect our schools.

I do not believe these killers were born with a gene that tells them to kill, that goes against the Biblical principles I adhere to. What wounds were beneath the surface in each of their lives that brought them to the point of committing such horrendous acts? Was there a point in time they could have been reached? It's time we become proactive in dealing with the ills that are corrupting our society by reaching out to those that are hurting and loving them, no matter how difficult it may be.

I understand these particular situations are extreme and horrendous. Tragedies like this go back to the book of Genesis with the story of the brothers Cain and Abel who were the sons of Adam and Eve. Cain became angry because

49

of the favor the Lord showed to Abel. God saw the anger or garbage in Cain's life and said,

"If you do what is right, will you not be accepted? But if you do not do what is right, sin is crouching at your door; it desires to have you, but you must rule over it."(Genesis 4:7)

God's warning didn't stop Cain, and he murdered his brother. Is sin crouching at your door? If so, where did it come from? More than likely, there is an open wound under the surface that God wants to heal. That wound may have been self-inflicted or caused by someone else. Honestly, it doesn't matter; the garbage is there either way.

Psalm 139:23,24 says,

"Search me, God, and know my heart; test me and know my anxious thoughts. See if there is any offensive way in me, and lead me in the way everlasting."

Will you make this your prayer today and open your heart to God as the only one who can heal the wound and take away your pain? It doesn't matter how many times you have messed up or walked away, His love is unfailing and available to you right now. Call out to Him, allow Him to do a deep work so that He can fulfill His plan for your life.

Chapter Six
Alone

In 2000 the movie *Castaway* was released with Tom Hanks starring as the fictional character Chuck Noland, a FedEx system engineer who traveled the world at a hectic pace. The beginning of the movie told how the job hindered any hope of a successful relationship he could have with his fiancé Kelly Fears, played by Helen Hunt. While on one of his many trips across the world, his plane went down during a violent storm which took the lives of everyone, with the exception of Noland. He lived on an island four years without seeing a person.

The movie was a huge success grossing $429 million and led to Hanks being nominated for Best Actor at the 73rd Academy Awards. I have watched the movie numerous times and find it fascinating that the vast majority of the scenes only have one character. Of course, the legend of Tom Hanks speaks for itself as one of the most significant actors of our time.

The theme of this entire movie hits home with a fear many have of being alone. The fear can be so consuming that it dictates the direction of lives. It causes those it dominates to settle in marriages, jobs, and relationships.

In the movie, you see the dramatic emotional and mental impact it has on the globe-trotting Chuck Noland when he is trapped alone without the ability to get to the next destination and job assignment.

Noland is eventually rescued and goes back to the life he had left and the people who thought he was dead. Not only had his world changed, but he had also changed. The things he had been forced to do to learn to survive had made him a different person. In the real world, production had to stop for a year while Hanks transformed the way he looked so he could portray the physical change in the character.

As a long-time business traveler, I learned to be alone and it doesn't bother me. It was normal for me to travel and eat alone in restaurants. During my stays, I would spend time with work associates and customers, but much of the time was by myself. It's been many years since I worked in an office environment and at this point in my career, I would struggle with the structure it requires.

The most joyous times in my life are when all of my family are together and my four absolutely wonderful and perfect grandchildren are running the show. Then there is my most productive time, in my office alone working, as I am now, writing this chapter.

JUST GOD & ME

There is another type of being alone that is required when we choose to Go Deep. You see, God does a deep work in our lives when we recognize that our relationship with Jesus is between each of us individually. It is not a group exercise. Jesus said in John 15:4-5,

"Remain in Me, as I also remain in you. No branch can bear fruit by itself; it must remain in the vine. Neither can you bear fruit unless you remain in Me. I am the vine; you are the branches. If you remain in Me and I in you, you will bear much fruit; apart from me you can do nothing."

The emphasis here is the singular source: Jesus is the vine, the source, and to be a productive Christ follower, we must remain completely attached to Him alone. He doesn't say if all will abide in Him, He is speaking to each of us independently.

There are times when God calls His people together to worship, fellowship, pray, and to agree. His most extensive work comes in the solitude of being alone with our Creator. Often this goes against our human desire to be accepted and connected with people and to gain approval.

God's desire is for an intimate, personal relationship with each of us. It's only then we are able to truly hear His voice and receive all that He has for us beneath the surface of our lives.

You find in the gospels time and time again when Jesus would go away from the disciples to pray alone. When teaching on prayer in Matthew 6, His words speak volumes on being alone with God,

"But when you pray, go into your room, close the door and pray to your Father, who is unseen. Then your Father, who sees what is done in secret, will reward you." (v.6)

He then gives us the example of the Lord's Prayer. Have you ever thought of the power and the simplicity of the words spoken? Jesus taught us to be very specific when we approach the throne of God. In other words, get to the point.

One of the most powerful examples Jesus gives us of being alone with God was at Gethsemane. As He was preparing for His destiny, He went alone and prayed deep, desperate prayers. Mark's account in chapter 14 says,

"He took Peter, James, and John along with Him, and He began to be deeply distressed and troubled," and said, "My soul is overwhelmed with sorrow to the point of death."
(v.34)

Then when He was alone, the Scripture says,

"He fell to the ground and prayed that if possible, the hour might pass from Him. "Abba Father," He said, "everything is possible for You. Take this cup from Me. Yet not what I will but what you will." (v.35)

Luke's account in chapter 22 says,

"And being in anguish, He prayed more earnestly, and His sweat was like drops of blood falling to the ground." (v.44)

I want you to feel the intensity of Jesus as He called out to God, knowing that His destiny was about to be fulfilled. In His humanity, He felt the weight of the responsibility He had to mankind, it was overwhelming and intense. I would guess that few of us have been in such deep prayer that it overwhelmed us physically as it did our Lord.

Going deep is about connecting with God with intensity. It is about crying out to God as we move toward our purpose.

HE MADE ME TO BE ME

At a point in my personal journey, God directed me in my daily prayer when alone with Him to pray for forgiveness, for healing, for the Holy Spirit, for change, and to be used.

At first, I prayed that God would change me to be a different person. Through time, God impacted me with the knowledge that He made me to be me, and He had a plan for my life. As flawed as each of us is, He created us for a reason and not to be someone else. It was when I was alone with God that He spoke these words to me, into the deep caverns of my soul.

Psalm 139 says it powerfully,

"For YOU created MY inmost being; YOU knit ME together in my mother's womb. I praise YOU because I am fearfully and wonderfully made; YOUR works are wonderful." (v.13, 14)

I want you to notice the words "inmost being." Catch this, when God created you, it was intentional and purposeful. It was a deep work in your mother's womb, and He made you from the inside. He created your soul, and it was wonderfully done.

Our two sons are 15 months apart. We didn't necessarily plan to have them so close, but God did. Trust me, two energetic, competitive little boys kept us on our toes. Now, as they are in their 30's, it is more obvious than ever of what God's plan was. My sons, though different, have become best friends in life and their relationship today is an inspiration to many. My oldest son Michael is a man of many talents, he loves his family, and is a wonderful father to his two incredible children, Reagan and Landry.

Then there is Matt, who is equally talented but in very different ways than Michael. He has two beautiful little girls, Madison and Harper, whom he loves deeply and is also a wonderful father. I was thrilled to have two sons and today, I reflect proudly on the men they are and recognize that even though we didn't necessarily plan the timing, God did, and His plan is perfect.

September 16, 2017, was another milestone for our family. It was the day I walked our third child, my beautiful daughter Amanda, down the aisle and gave her to her husband, Craig.

Eight years after Matt was born, God had another plan, and He created a perfect baby girl. I have said two things during my little girl's life: she was easier than the boys but far more expensive and there would never be a man good enough for her. I had to humbly retract those words at her wedding because God blessed her with the one who was good enough. I think of how God purposed her so differently than her brothers as a teacher whose heart is so filled with compassion.

We have an accountant, Michael, married to Bethany, a Physician's Assistant. A sales professional, Matt, married to Elise, a nutritionist. A teacher, Amanda married to a coach, Craig. I am equally proud of each of my children and their spouses and thank God that He chose to create them for a specific reason and gave me the honor to be their father. Of course, I could write a completely separate book on the gift of grandchildren. By the way, have I shown you their latest pictures?

My point is, as my family grew and developed, I watched not only my children, but my grandchildren establish their God-given identity. It was then my daily prayer changed and I began to pray, "God make me into who YOU designed ME to be." We are all guilty of disobeying God, I certainly am. Tragically, some will give up on their destiny. Unfortunately, many times people give up because those in their lives have given up on them. When alone with God, it forces us to see no one else but Him. When there are people and personalities in view, it can cloud our sight.

If you don't know what your life's plan is, pray that God will reveal His plan for your life. If you are like me and feel like you have failed and missed God's plan, please hear me, *it's not too late*. A favorite passage of many is found in Jeremiah 29:11,

"For I know the plans I have for you," declares the Lord, "plans to prosper you and not to harm you, plans to give you hope and a future."

No matter the route taken to get there, know that it is His desire for all of us to have hope and a future and find success in Him.

SUCCESS = FAVOR

Our culture views success very differently than God does. We look at athletes who have reached the pinnacle of the sports world and we may think, "If only I could jump that high or hit the ball that far or catch a pass like that, THEN I would know success." Perhaps we look at an actor or musician who fills the newspaper headlines, television, and movie screens and we wish, "If only I could sing or act like that, THEN I would know success." Sadly, we see it in some Christian leaders who think, "If only I could preach like that or if I could pastor that church, THEN I would know success." We find ourselves striving to be like someone else, and since we can't, we look for their favor.

When you Go Deep with God, you understand the true measure of success is having God's favor, and it becomes your heart's desire and intense focus.

There are powerful promises in the Bible about God's favor, Psalm 5:12,

"Surely, Lord, You bless the righteous, You surround them with Your favor as with a shield."

Tie this to the armor of God in Ephesians 6 with the "breastplate of righteousness in place" and to "take up the shield of faith."

What is the purpose of a shield and a breastplate? They are protectors, and as God's armor, we are to put them on and take them up, which brings righteousness and gains favor from God.

Remember, breaking through the surface to Go Deep requires humility and brokenness. According to Proverbs 3:34 it is to the humble that He shows favor. When you stop looking for man's approval and favor and passionately focus on pleasing God, you will find His favor and your God-given destiny.

LONELINESS

I shared in the introduction about the journey the Lord has taken me in the deep. I will tell you it is difficult, and even though your desire is to connect personally with God, there are times of extreme loneliness. Our human nature is to be connected with people. To Go Deep with God forces a separation so that we will develop a complete dependence on Him.

There are times God will go quiet, and at times you will not even feel Him with you. The test is there so we will build our faith and trust in Him. We know He is unseen and when He is quiet, doubt can creep in and try to convince us He isn't there, but He is, He never leaves nor forsakes us.

The 23rd Psalm is a passage of restoration written by David. In the very beginning of the chapter, the declaration is made,

"The Lord is my shepherd, I lack nothing."

Before we move any deeper, we must confess that He is our only source and there is nothing else we have or could need that anyone or anything can supply. The greatest failure is when success takes hold of us, and we begin to believe we are the reason.

INVISIBLE & DESPERATE

To Go Deep means to be alone, beneath the surface, with total dependence on God. You may feel invisible, just know it is part of God's plan in doing a deep work in your life. It is during this time that you are growing your faith and building your trust. It's a powerful and necessary lesson to discover all that God has for us. Remember, it is in the desert, in the valley of life where you find God, where you hear His voice.

In my personal journey in the deep, I often asked the Lord when it would end. When would I arrive at my destiny? It was only when I realized that if I truly wanted to know God and be all that He made me to be, the journey could never end. Pursuing God's will and purpose was my destiny. You see, when I am in the deep, I am desperate and I am crying out to God. If I leave that place, I will leave my desperation, and I never want to do that.

The picture I mentioned in my office with Psalm 143:8 inscribed is one I took. It is at a place near our home in the country where there are beautiful red stag deer. I stumbled on them early one morning on a drive, and they mesmerized me. The picture is a deer standing alone near the water, and it reminds me of Psalm 42:1 which says,

"As the deer pants for streams of water, so my soul pants for You, my God."

Oh, may we always be as desperate for the Lord as the deer are for the water.

It is my prayer that you do not fear being alone with God. It may mean leaving people or things behind. The reward is a full life, a life where destiny is fulfilled.

Chapter Six – Alone

Chapter Seven
The Legend of Kalopin

A story is told of a nineteenth-century Chickasaw Indian chief who was born with a deformed foot, so the people called him Kalopin, which means Reelfoot. When he became Chief, he was unhappy because he could not find the woman of his dreams among his people. Unfortunately for him, internet dating sites were not available, so he headed south where he heard there were many beautiful women.

Reelfoot arrived in the territory of a Choctaw Chief, Copiah, who had a beautiful daughter named Laughing Eyes. The princess immediately won the heart of the young chief. Reelfoot asked her father for her hand in marriage and was denied. Chief Copiah did not want his daughter to marry someone who was handicapped, especially one who was not of the same tribe.

The legend goes on to say that the father called on the Great Spirit who told Reelfoot that if he took Laughing Eyes, he would cause a great earthquake and it would flood the land. The young chief was not going to be denied from being with the love of his life, so he stole her and took her home to marry. During the wedding celebration, as promised, the earth rocked, and the great Mississippi River flooded the land. A beautiful lake was formed and is said to be the gravesite of Chief Reelfoot, his bride, and his people.

So, there you have it, an Indian version of Romeo and Juliet. Over the years, the story has been disproven, and for the record, I do not believe in Indian legends. What is true is that Reelfoot Lake is in northwest Tennessee and was formed by the New Madrid earthquakes in the early 1800s. The original name was the Red Foot River, and it was simply through a misinterpretation of an early map that the 'd' was separated into an 'e' and 'l' and thus became Reelfoot Lake. The true story is not as sensational as the Indian legend, and if you were to see the lake, you could imagine it as the graveyard of the love-starved chief. It is filled with lots of tree stumps and beautiful vegetation. It is so stumpy that the only boats allowed are canoe style with small inboard motors. The danger is that one of the many stumps, when hit, could cause permanent damage to a nice fishing boat.

Reelfoot Lake has fond memories for me; I spent many Saturday mornings there as a young boy fishing with my dad. I loved the story of the great earthquake. I would picture a forest with giant trees that now only had the very tops displayed above the murky water. It is a fisherman's dream due to the quantity of fish regularly caught. We would use a trolling motor to pull the boat as close to the trees stumps as possible and drop a double hooked line down among the many lily pads. It was simple fishing, no casting, just drop your line, and it was not unusual to quickly see the sinker go below water with fish on both hooks.

WATER AND THE BIBLE

The Bible contains many true stories of bodies of water that have significance for believers. In the Old Testament, we know that in order for the children of Israel to obtain their freedom from Pharaoh, God parted the Red Sea. After they had crossed, the waters swallowed the Egyptian army. We also know that at the end of the 40 years, God stopped the flow of water from the Jordan River at flood stage. The Priests carrying the ark of the covenant stepped to the edge and immediately the water was pushed back. It began to flow again only when all the Israelites were on the other side.

The story of Noah building the ark and God flooding the land is a favorite of children ministries everywhere, as is Jonah in the belly of the great fish for three days and three nights. The storylines of water are chock-full of life lessons for believers — themes of obedience vs. rebellion, wandering, and false gods. There are leadership lessons as Jonah returned to fulfill his purpose and as Moses passed the torch to Joshua.

The New Testament continues with more themes around bodies of water. We know Jesus spent much time teaching near water and working miracles such as feeding the five thousand on the shore of the Sea of Galilee. He chose fisherman to be part of His twelve.

A story that has been especially real to me in my latest journey of faith is found in Matthew 14. It tells of Jesus, sending the disciples ahead in a boat while He went alone to pray. Do you see the continual connection of Jesus being alone with God within the timeline of working miracles?

When He was ready to join His followers, He saw they were in the midst of a rocky ride. It didn't stop Him, and He didn't need another boat to get to them, He just took off across the lake. So, here goes Peter, always the impulsive one, saying,

"Lord, if it's You, tell me to come to You on the water."
(Matthew 14:28)

Jesus responded simply,

"Come"

Peter did and began to walk toward the Lord. He then did what we do so often as Christians, he took his eyes off Jesus and sank. Why was it so hard to keep focused on the one who just took five loaves of bread and two fish and fed a multitude and had left-overs? It was because of the wind. What's interesting to me, the Scripture doesn't say he was knocked over by the wind, which would cause him to sink, it says,

"When he SAW the wind, he was afraid and, beginning to sink, cried out, 'Lord save me!'" (v.30)

No wonder the Lord responded,

"You of little faith, why did you doubt?" (v.31)

He didn't sink because the wind caught up with him, he sank because of his lack of faith which was overcome with fear. I wonder if Peter was more fearful of the wind that he saw or the water under his feet. Both are powerful forces that can create fear, but Jesus doesn't panic at either one. In Matthew, He was walking on water, and in Mark 4, He calmed the winds just by telling them to be quiet. The same Jesus is more than able today to work miracles in our lives if we will just keep our eyes and focus on Him alone.

ROOTED

When you Go Deep beneath the surface of your life, you will find out what the Psalmist means when he says about the merchants of the sea,

"They saw the works of the Lord, His wonderful deeds in the deep." (107:24)

This passage greatly intrigues me and causes me to want to understand more about what God does as He develops us to be all that He has made us to be.

Think back to Reelfoot Lake and the trees stretching out of the water. These large bald cypresses rooted in the bottom of the lake form the landscape. The water lilies which seemingly float on top are also rooted like the trees in the soil, and some species of fish will feed off of them. Paul writing in Colossians 2 says,

"So then, just as you have received Christ Jesus as Lord, continue to live your lives in Him, rooted and built up in Him, strengthened in the faith as you were taught, and overflowing with thankfulness." (6-7)

It's important to understand the context of what Paul is saying in this letter to the church in Colossae. It had been established during Paul's third missionary journey while in Ephesus. A Colossian named Epaphras had received the gospel there and taken it back to his home and shared the good news, and the church was established. Yet another example of the church being built from the outside in.

Paul is writing the letter while he is in prison in Rome. It begins with encouragement and thanksgiving before he gives warning against false teaching. He writes,

"See to it that no one takes you captive through hollow and deceptive philosophy, which depends on human tradition and the elemental spiritual forces of this world rather than on Christ." (v.8)

The point Paul is making, no matter what else you hear or what society may bring attention to, if it doesn't line up with the gospel of Jesus Christ, then stay away from it and do not allow anyone to suck you in. We live in a day where there is a significant amount of teaching that is questionable. Because of this, we must be individually rooted and able to discern what truly is of God.

The definition of the word rooted is "firmly implanted." In our previous home, we had several large live oak trees that surrounded our property. We lived in this house for 20 years and watched as each year they would become more and more majestic. Their roots were firmly entrenched in the ground and immovable. It was necessary each year to have the branches pruned back to avoid disease and to keep them healthy and vibrant. It was also necessary during the hot, dry months of summer to make sure the root system was watered regularly. It was not uncommon during a storm to see limbs break off and some neighbors lose their trees because they had not been maintained and were not prepared for the winds.

It's when we are alone with God that He is strengthening the root system in our lives. Just like my live oaks, He regularly cuts away the unnecessary branches to keep us healthy and prunes the necessary ones to allow new growth. When a tree is pruned, it will look really bare and empty, but when the new growth begins, it will take the tree to a new level of development. It is the same with each of us. In John 15:1-2 Jesus said,

"I am the true vine, and the Father is the gardener. He cuts off every branch in me that bears no fruit, while every branch that does bear fruit, He prunes so it will be even more fruitful."

Some of the branches that are cut from our lives could be garbage from the past or from sin. It may be things that at one time were healthy and productive but now their season is over, and yet we continue to hold on. Until we allow God to cut and prune, we cannot move on to greater things.

Back to the passage in Colossians 2, where Paul is saying that we are to have Jesus firmly implanted in our lives, I like the way the NLT says,

"Let your roots grow down into Him, and let your lives be built on Him." (v.7)

Paul goes on to say,

"Then your faith will grow strong in the truth you were
taught."

This is a critical piece that cannot be neglected as you
Go Deep. It's not enough to expose the garbage and get rid
of it; you must also establish God's Word as the source for
all you do and who you are.

POWER SOURCE

After Pattillo Higgins at Spindletop Hill changed the
history of oil production, it continued to evolve with
unprecedented amounts of onshore drilling. In the late 1800s
and early 1900s, oil companies began to drill offshore deep
under the surface of bodies of water. Today, there are over
1300 offshore oil rigs across the world with 184 alone in the
Gulf of Mexico. They explore for and extract petroleum
which lies in rock formations beneath the seabed where there
are untapped energy resources.

Paul was again speaking to the church at Corinth in
1 Corinthians 2 and letting it be known that within himself
he was weak and overcome with fear when he came to them
to share the gospel. In verses 1-5, he wants it to be known
that there is nothing he could legitimately share without the
Spirit's power. He was emphatic in letting them know that it
was not his words but God's. A true test for someone who
comes as a messenger for God is to determine if the focus is
on them or Jesus?

When roots are established in God's Word, there is a power source that is available to each of us to equip us and empower us to live the life God has planned for us. Paul writes,

"'What no eye has seen, what no ear has heard, and what no human mind has conceived' - the things God has prepared for those who love Him - these are the things God has revealed to us by His Spirit." (v.9-10)

Get ahold of this promise, hold onto it like nothing else. Let's move on with what Paul is saying. It gets even better.

"The Spirit searches all things, even the deep things of God. For who knows a person's thoughts except their own spirit within them? In the same way, no one knows the thoughts of God except the Spirit of God. What we have received is not the spirit of the world, but the Spirit who is from God, so that we may understand what God has freely given us. This is what we speak, not in words taught us by human wisdom but in words taught by the Spirit, explaining spiritual realities with Spirit-taught words. The person without the Spirit does not accept things that come from the Spirit of God but considers them foolishness and cannot understand them because they are discerned only through the Spirit. The person with the Spirit makes judgments about all things, but such a person is not subject to merely human judgments, for, 'Who has known the mind of the Lord so as to instruct Him?' But we have the mind of Christ." (v.10-16)

There you go, Paul is explaining why so many Christians struggle with understanding God's Word. We try to do it within our own power, and it's not possible. He has given His Spirit, so we can understand His plan for us. It's up to each of us to then allow the Holy Spirit to take control of our lives; sadly, many do not. Could this be a reason why so many churches are trying to grab hold of every new fad to draw people? Is it because they have lost hold of the power source God has given us or is it that some are denying it even exists today? Paul warns us as he gave instructions to Timothy with these words about who to watch for, they will,

"Having a form of godliness but denying its power. Have nothing to do with such people." (2 Timothy 3:5)

When you Go Deep and are rooted in the Word of God, you have access to His power source, the Holy Spirit, to bring understanding and discernment.

LIFE

I must admit, the closest I have been to view the wonders of what lies beneath the surface of the ocean was at a visit to an aquarium and on the view from a glass bottom boat. Maybe you are one who loves to deep sea dive, or like me, have friends that do. Their stories are magical as they describe their experiences. They talk of the incredible schools of fish and the beautiful vegetation. Some (me) fear going underwater and dying, which can certainly happen. In reality, marine life consists of the plants, animals, and organisms that produce much of the oxygen we breathe. There is life in the deep.

In the beginning chapter about redemption, I wrote about the full life that Jesus promises us in John 10:10. Unfortunately, some Christians appear dead before they actually die. As a kid, raised in the church, I was scared to death of Romans 6:23 which says,

"The wages of sin is death…"

Stop, that's as far I could go. The rest of the verse is the promise of the gift of God through Jesus, but I couldn't get there. I was so afraid that if I sinned, there would be a bolt of lightning that would come down from heaven and I would end up charcoal. In reality, I proved my interpretation of the Scripture wrong by sinning and still waking up every morning.

What I now know is that to be spiritually dead is far worse than physical death. Sin causes separation from God which makes us part of the walking dead. The good news, we do not have to be burdened down with the sins and anxieties of this life. We can choose "life to the full" promised to each of us.

As I shared earlier, I grew up in a very strict Christian home where everything our culture offered was a sin, so we couldn't participate in it. What the 60's and 70's offered was like going to Disneyland compared to what society offers today. Labeling sin was much more prevalent than in comparison to today where it is hard to distinguish what society believes is right or wrong.

My mother was raised as a Pentecostal preacher's kid and brought much of her upbringing into our home. Up until her dying day, she had a fierce love for God, and like my grandparents, was devoted to praying daily for all of her family. I thank God for that heritage that I know has brought me through more than I can ever imagine. Her upbringing also brought the legalism of the day, which honestly caused a lot of confusion and bondage. When you see someone held captive by legalism, it's hard to see them living life to the full, and it's almost impossible to see grace.

In Romans 6, Paul helps us to understand this balance between sin and grace when he writes,

"What shall we say, then? Shall we go on sinning so that grace may increase? By no means! We are those who have died to sin; how can we live in it any longer?" (v.1-2)

So, the million-dollar question for many today, what is sin? Verse 12 says do not let sin,

"reign in your mortal body so that you obey its evil desires."

and verse 14 says,

"Sin shall no longer be your master…"

When you look closely at the depth of this passage, you can take from it that sin is whatever controls us and becomes our master other than God himself. It makes it hard to then put a label on particular "things" as was done when

I was a kid. Please don't misunderstand me, the Bible speaks very specifically about issues that do not please God and separates us from Him. Galatians 5:19-21 says,

"The acts of the flesh are obvious; sexual immorality, impurity, and debauchery; idolatry and witchcraft; hatred, discord, jealousy, fits of rage, selfish ambition, dissensions, factions and envy; drunkenness, orgies and the like."

and he goes on to say,

"...those who live like this will not inherit the kingdom of God."

Sin has become such a complex issue in our society today, especially in the church, when in reality it should not be. As we Go Deep under the surface of our lives and find grace, we then find life.

"And if the Spirit of Him who raised Jesus from the dead is living in you, He who raised Christ from the dead will also give life to your mortal bodies because of His Spirit who lives in you. Therefore, brothers and sisters, we have an obligation - but it is not to the flesh, to live according to it. For if you live according to the flesh, you will die; but if by the Spirit you put to death the misdeeds of the body, you will live." (Romans 8:11-13)

As you go to God in desperation, wanting all that He has for you, let nothing separate you from Him.

"No, in all these things we are more than conquerors through Him who loves us. For I am convinced that neither death nor life, neither angels nor demons, neither the present nor the future, nor any powers, neither height nor depth, nor anything else in all creation, will be able to separate us from the love of God that is in Christ Jesus our Lord." (Romans 8:37-39)

FREEDOM

My deep-sea diving friends talk about the great expanse of their adventures. They feel limitless as they explore, free from the world above the surface. They experience the mysteries of the deep and the beauty of God's creation.

I have met many people who will not give their life to Christ because they fear what they will have to give up and lose what they believe is freedom. They associate Christianity with a list of do's and don'ts, like being in prison. In the Old Testament, people were governed by the law, in the New Testament, we are freed by grace. Some may look at that as a license to do whatever without restrictions. Not at all, we are free because we have confessed our sins and left the old life behind.

"Therefore, if anyone is in Christ, the new creation has come: The old has gone, the new is here!"
(2 Corinthians 5:17)

I love the exclamation point the NIV puts at the end, as it should be, because it's exciting, we are free! Jesus said it himself in John 8:36,

"So, if the Son sets you free, you will be free indeed."

When you Go Deep and find spiritual freedom, it is not about what you can't do; it's about the freedom you have to be all God made you to be, it's liberating. When you find that freedom, your purpose, plans, and priorities change. I think of those raised in other religions who find Christ and are excommunicated from their families, and some are even put to death.

I recently met a man whose ministry goes into Muslim countries in Africa. They have found soft clay and open hearts and have seen many come to Christ. He told me there are many threats to their lives, yet he and his partners have made the decision, if necessary, to give their lives for others to know Jesus. These stories have been told for decades and honestly back to the early apostles who gave it all to spread the gospel. Paul, the greatest apostle who wrote much of the New Testament, had an encounter in the deep with God and wrote while in chains,

"For to me, to live is Christ and to die is gain."
Philippians 1:21

Can you grasp that? Someone was willing to give his life, and he did, for a cause that has changed the world.

You now have a glimpse of the wonderful deeds in the deep that God has for you. To understand what it means to Go Deep is to become rooted in the Word of God and allow the Holy Spirit to give you understanding. It is my prayer that you will begin to experience the full life and freedom promised to those who believe.

Chapter Eight
A Bag of Potatoes

The process of writing this book has been like nothing I could have ever imagined. It has been exhilarating when words just begin to flow, especially after those times when I was "stuck." It has been emotional and I felt very raw when reminded of different parts of my story.

I feel like writing has been a part of me since I was a boy, yet to this point, this is the furthest I have come to completing a book. As I started and put together a plan, I wondered if I would have enough to say or if anyone would read it. At this point, neither of those questions matter, it is completely in God's hands.

The process has certainly been a journey within itself. There have been disappointments and times of doubt that have tried to settle in. It's during those times I am reminded of the story of Peter in his attempt to walk on water and how I must remain laser-focused only on Jesus. As I write, I continually find times when the points I am sharing are very much needed by me.

I also have a confession to make: what I am doing in writing this book at this time in my life doesn't really make sense. There are other important things that need focus and attention. It's really hard to explain to people, so I don't try, I just continue. I am so incredibly blessed to have a supportive wife who, like I said earlier, doesn't always understand but always believes.

I know with everything in me that God has created the concept of Go Deep; it's not mine, it's His. It's up to me to trust and obey. So, that's what I am doing, and the journey continues. I hold fast to when Paul says to "press on" in Philippians 2. I am able to do it because of the markers in my life, the times in my past when God had proven himself faithful to my family when what we were doing didn't always make sense. In fact, I can honestly say, He has never failed us. Oh, there are plenty of times I have failed or gotten ahead of God, but that's not the case now, I know because of those markers.

When you Go Deep, and God makes you into who He designed you to be, he will inevitably bring you to a calling to do something that is bigger than you. A plan that can only be done by God through those who are fully devoted to Him. Such was the case with the Israelites as they came to the end of their journey, now led by Joshua. As they prepared to enter the promised land, the Bible says,

"Joshua told the people, 'Consecrate yourselves, for tomorrow the Lord will do amazing things among you.'"
(Joshua 3:5)

That's where we are; God is calling us to get ready because He is going to do "amazing things." Hang on, it only gets better.

CROSSING THE JORDAN

There was only one thing standing between the Israelites and the end of their journey, the Jordan River. In the last chapter, I wrote about how the Lord stopped the flow of water while at flood stage. The story continues,

"The priests who carried the ark of the covenant of the Lord stopped in the middle of the Jordan and stood on dry ground, while all Israel passed by until the whole nation completed the crossing on dry ground." (Joshua 3:17)

The Lord then told Joshua to do something I find very interesting and meaningful. He chose a man from each of the 12 tribes and had them go back to the middle of the Jordan where the priests were standing and to take up twelve stones. Mind you, the word stone may be a little deceiving due to the fact that they were told to put them on their shoulders, perhaps boulders may be a better description. The stones were taken to Gilgal, their first camp on that side of the Jordan and set up as memorials.

Joshua told the Israelites,

"In the future when your descendants ask their parents, 'What do these stones mean?' tell them, 'Israel crossed the Jordan on dry ground.' For the Lord dried up the Jordan before you until you had crossed over. The Lord your God did to the Jordan what he had done to the Red Sea when he dried it up before us until we had crossed over. He did this so that all the peoples of the earth might know the hand of the Lord is powerful and so that you might always fear the Lord your God." (Joshua 4:21-24)

PURPOSE OF MARKERS

It's important to note that God's purpose is more than the actual event that the marker was built for. It certainly meets the need of the moment, but it's bigger than that. When you believe the Bible is more than a book of stories, you then understand it is full of markers for us today. **God uses markers to build our faith so that we will continue to follow Him**. Hebrews 11 says,

"Now faith is confidence in what we hope for and assurance about what we do not see. This is what the ancients were commended for." (v.1-2)

The chapter then goes through a Who's Who of Old Testament heroes providing markers for us, meant to build our faith and deepen our knowledge of the power of God. Chapter 12 then lays it out,

"Therefore, since we are surrounded by such a great cloud of witnesses, let us throw off everything that hinders and the sin that so easily entangles. And let us run with perseverance the race marked out for us, fixing our eyes on Jesus, the pioneer and perfecter of faith." (v.1-2)

I love the story of Bartimaeus, as told in Mark 10. It's a story of faith demonstrated by a man who was physically blind. In our culture today, he might be considered homeless and a nuisance to society. Obviously, he disgusted those who saw him, and to think, he had the audacity to shout,

"Jesus, Son of David, have mercy on me!" (v.47)

It raised the ire of the crowd even more. That didn't stop him, and he continued to shout,

"Son of David, have mercy on me!" (v.48)

Get this, the blind beggar believed that Jesus could touch him even when society had no hope for him and considered him a problem. The Scriptures do not tell us about Bartimaeus' past other than he was the son of a man named Timaeus. I have to wonder what brought him to this point. Had everyone around him written him off? What we do know, he had hope in what he heard about Jesus. I am sure he was hanging around crowds and heard the stories of healings and miracles, markers. Maybe, he saw this as his last chance, I don't know, but it caused him to cry out for mercy persistently. Think about it, in his desperation he would not be denied his chance to meet the Son of God. My friends, I call that faith. In fact, more importantly, Jesus did and simply said to those around him,

"Call him."

When Jesus spoke those words, the tone of the fickle crowd changed, and now they were telling him,

"Cheer up! On your feet! He's calling you."

Perhaps you are reading this and you are discouraged and feel like everyone around you has deserted you. If so, summon every ounce of faith you have and reach out to Him in the place you are and hear these words, "Cheer up! On your feet! HE is calling YOU!" My guess is, if you Go Deep, there are markers in your past that will ignite your faith.

Bartimaeus did something else that I believe is important in declaring his faith,

"He threw his cloak aside and jumped to his feet."

It was the coat of a beggar, and even before he could physically see, he was stepping out in faith, believing his miracle was in reach. He was getting rid of everything that, "hindered and entangled" him.

Jesus knew what he needed, not only because it was obvious that Bartimaeus was blind, it was important for him to tell Jesus his need,

"Rabbi, I want to see." "Go," said Jesus, "your faith has healed you."

Don't miss this, after he was healed, Bartimaeus didn't run away,

"He received his sight and followed Jesus along the road."

This was a marker not only in the life of this changed man, but to you and me today. God will meet our needs as we step out in faith and it is imperative that we follow Him down this road called life.

God uses markers to demonstrate his power -

"He did this so that all the peoples of the earth might know
that the hand of the Lord is powerful..." (Joshua 4:24)

The miracle of the Jordan was just the latest example
of God demonstrating His power to the Israelites. When you
go back to Joshua chapter 2, you read the story of Rahab the
prostitute and the two spies sent out by Joshua to scout out
Jericho before the Israelites crossed the Jordan. Rahab made
a momentous decision to align herself with God's people to
the point of endangering herself and her family. Her choice
was to either put her trust in the king of Jericho or believe
the stories she had heard of God's power working through
the Israelites; she chose the latter. Think about this: there was
no cable news network, no newspaper or radio, yet the
stories of what God had done during the 40 years of the
journey had spread.

She said to the spies,

"I know that the Lord has given you this land and that a
great fear of you has fallen on us, so that all who live in this
country are melting in fear because of you. We have heard
how the Lord dried up the water of the Red Sea for you
when you came out of Egypt, and what you did to Sihon
and Og, the two kings of the Amorites east of the Jordan,
whom you completely destroyed. When we heard of it, our
hearts melted in fear and everyone's courage failed because
of you, for the Lord your God is God in heaven above and
on the earth below." (Joshua 2:9-11)

Make no mistake about it, when God moves, He leaves markers and the word spreads. The reason, just like Rahab, becomes a decision to believe that the "Lord your God is God" or continue to serve other gods. The same decision remains for us today.

You may say, well this is the Old Testament. We do not hear of waters parting today or even the miracles we heard of in the New Testament, such as the healing of blind Bartimaeus, Peter walking on the water, or Jesus calming the storm. If you choose to believe the Bible is the infallible Word of God, then how do you deny His power today?

In John 14, as Jesus was preparing the disciples for His departure, He was addressing their confusion and honestly their fears. He is telling them that the Holy Spirit will be with us forever (v.16). There are strong instructions to keep His commands (v.15) and Jesus even explains how the world will not accept Him or understand because He is not seen. He promises that because we know Him, He lives with us and will be in us (v.17). When you go back a few verses, Jesus speaks to the question of His power available to us today when He says in verse 12,

"Very truly I tell you, whoever believes in Me will do the works I have been doing, and they will do even greater things than these, because I am going to the Father."

I do not see a statute of limitations on this passage or any other. I understand that the world is unbelieving and even many in the church. I understand that there has been abuse and misinterpretation of the Scriptures, but those things do not change the Word of God. Isaiah 40:8 says,

"...the Word of our God endures forever."

Friends do not limit God by believing He is no longer powerful. He uses his power, just like He did with Rahab, so people will hear and make the decision to follow Him. Hear the words of the Psalmist,

"Among the gods there is none like You, Lord; no deeds can compare with Yours. All the nations You have made will come and worship before You Lord; they will bring glory to Your name. For You are great and do marvelous deeds, You alone are God." (Psalm 86:8)

There you go, as we continue to Go Deep, we have even more assurance of the "marvelous deeds," He will do because He is God.

Markers represent our legacy - The Lord spoke these words to Joshua,

"As I was with Moses, so I will be with you." (Joshua 1:5)

Can you imagine what is going through Joshua's mind, as well as the Children of Israel? Moses was the one whom God had chosen to lead them out of captivity and now he was gone. What incredible sandals to fill, yet God was promising to do the same through Joshua as He had through Moses. Their roles and responsibilities were different in God's plan, but what was required was the same, the blessing of God. You see, Moses had left a legacy of markers for Joshua to see and follow.

I remember a day when I worked for a large corporation and we were called into a conference room where it was announced there was a change in leadership. The person in charge was moving to take over the largest segment in our company, a momentous task. She was a leader who had great influence on my career and many others. She was dynamic and had the God-given ability to get the most out of people and the record of her success was superior. In that environment, I had worked for and seen many in the same or equivalent roles and none had her success nor the level of respect from the people. After she made the announcement, she then said she was being replaced by another leader within our group. At that point, I had never met this man and had not even seen him until that day. When he began to speak, it was evident he was more of a quiet soul without the dynamic of his predecessor. His first words were, "I have to admit, I am a little bit scared." I got it, it was hard to replace someone who had left such a legacy. I tend to believe this was what Joshua may have felt and why God said to him three times,

"Be strong and courageous." He even said, "...Do not be afraid; do not be discouraged for the Lord your God will be with you wherever you go." (Joshua 1:9)

The new leader of our division was a good man, his style was different, but he made his own path. Ironically, over the next few years, he rose to the highest level in the entire company. I got to know him and watched him during those years, and I saw a quiet confidence begin to rise up in him. He didn't become a different person, he just grew. I truly believe one reason he grew was that he had been left a legacy to follow and there were markers he could look back on. It's important to remember that markers reflect a time in the past, so they must be kept in perspective.

As a public speaker, I give a presentation called, "Rear-View Mirror," I talk about my first car, a 68 Chevrolet Impala that had been passed down through my family. It was a beast, but it was mine and I loved it. It had one flaw that was tough to overcome: the rear-view mirror kept falling off the front windshield. You might think something that small shouldn't matter, but it does. Without it, you lose your balance and driving becomes difficult. With it, you are able to glance back and see where you came from, and if necessary, adjust accordingly. The key word is "glance." If you stare in it too long, then you have the possibility of missing a turn, or even worse, hitting someone in front of you.

It was important for Joshua to glance back on the legacy of Moses while moving forward. By doing so, his faith grew and gave him the assurance that the God who spoke through a burning bush and turned a staff into a snake and then back to a staff, would do the same for him. Remember, it was Moses who led the Israelites at the beginning of the journey as God opened the Red Sea, but it was Joshua who led them across the Jordan River as God pushed back the water. It was Joshua who led the army and the priests around the walls of Jericho seven times until they came tumbling down and they conquered the city and possessed the land. Moses began the journey, Joshua finished it.

Legacy building should be a lifetime pursuit and the result of the full life Jesus promises us. It is my passion that my kids will look back on a life well lived and their father as one who,

> "...fought the good fight and finished the race and kept the faith." (2 Timothy 4:7)

I want to leave markers they can look back on and through faith, they will know there is nothing our powerful God can't do.

WHAT ABOUT THE POTATOES?

At this point, you may be wondering about the title of this chapter and thinking, "What does any of this have to do with potatoes?" So let me tell you. A bag of potatoes represents a significant marker for my family. There have been many, but this is one I have shared countless times over the past 25 years.

In 1993, my family had the opportunity to return home to Dallas. I had been serving in youth ministry in Waco, Texas and God had opened a significant door to start a church. It was a huge step of faith for us to leave our comfort zone and security, but we knew it was God's plan for our lives. I left my position and salary and headed back home to begin to reach out to people and start the process of starting the new church. Our boys were in elementary school, so we made the decision for my family to stay until school was out and I would live with my parents until they could join me.

Pastoring is one of the hardest and most misunderstood jobs out there and starting a church from scratch with very little financial support at times seemed impossible. I started valet parking cars, spending deep nights at a hospital emergency room. It allowed me to keep my days open to do the necessary things for the new church. That time in my life helped prepare me for what we are doing today. It was difficult and rewarding, filled with blessings and disappointments, but we knew it was what God wanted us to do.

My wife, LeeAnne, is an extremely frugal person. As I mentioned earlier, she was raised in the home of school teachers and they were extremely disciplined with how they had to handle money. Me, not so much. I tend to be more freewheeling and have been known to impulse buy. Again, I am thankful for the balance God gave me in my wife.

One thing we don't do together is shop, for the sake of our marriage. Well, it's not quite that serious, but we have learned through the years that it's OK to avoid pain. For me, the pain is spending hours in a store going through every item on the shelf to find the one that might be marked down less than the others. Then there are the coupons, the endless coupons that have honestly, through the years, saved us the equivalent of Fort Knox. For LeeAnne, the pain is me, shopping, period. I can spend half the time in the store by myself and get the same items and for some strange reason, I always pay more. How does that happen?

One night while I was in Dallas and my family in Waco, I called home on this ancient piece of equipment called a landline telephone. It was before everyone had a cell phone and we couldn't have afforded it anyway. When LeeAnne answered the phone, I could tell she was down. My wife was made to be a mother and now a grandmother.

There is nothing more important to her than making sure her children and grandchildren have everything they need. She told me she had been to the store to buy a few things, which I am sure took hours, and decided to make chili. She put all the ingredients in the basket and added a bag of potatoes. While she wandered around the store, she decided she couldn't pay for the groceries, so she put everything back on the shelf, except the bag of potatoes.

She was telling me the story when the doorbell rang and ended our call. A short time later, she called and told me the rest of the story of the bag of potatoes. A lady from the church we had just left was at the door and told her God had laid on her heart to bring us some groceries. She went on to say that her Dad had started many churches in her lifetime, and she understood and wanted to bless us. The story could stop right there and be a good one, but it gets better. After LeeAnne thanked the kind lady for her generosity and she left, she began to take the items out of the bags. When she did, she found everything she had put back on the shelves, except the bag of potatoes. To her, it was God saying, it was going to be OK, He would provide.

You see, God knows our hearts and He knows exactly how to speak to us so we will know that He loves us. LeeAnne is the practical one and it is important to her for God to speak to her in practical ways. There was absolutely no denying it was God. I can be more of a wild visionary and would probably sleep in my car and eat bread crumbs if necessary. LeeAnne is different, thank God. It goes back to how He created our "inmost being," meaning He didn't have a cookie cutter to make us all the same, it was detail work.

For my wife, He knew what she needed because He had made her to be who she was.

This moment became a marker for us, especially LeeAnne, and strengthened our faith for the journey ahead. I have told this story many times over the years to people who were struggling in a situation. I have seen many tears well up in eyes because it was an encouraging word for them, a marker. Again, when God works in powerful ways, His purpose is more than just for the moment, it is for the days ahead and for others.

FAITH VS. TRUST

I consider myself a man of faith who believes there is nothing that God cannot do. I believe because of what the Bible tells me and because of the markers in my life. My struggle many times is to trust, even though I know He always has and can, I still find myself wondering IF He will. How can someone with faith not trust? It's because trust requires us to relinquish control, and therein lies the problem. It's those times when faith battles the feeling of being irresponsible.

Like most men, I feel my God-given responsibility to make sure my family is taken care of and they have all they need. My answer is found in Proverbs 3:5, which says,

"Trust in the Lord with all your heart and lean not on your own understanding; in all your ways acknowledge Him, and He shall direct your paths."

There you have it, in order to Go Deep in your life, it requires complete surrender, not partial surrender, everything. It's when the excavator has broken through your stubborn will and pride and your focus turns to acknowledging Him. Still, God doesn't make us mindless robots; just the opposite. The verse says, He will "direct your path" which means when decisions need to be made, He is leading you while He is providing for you.

Just like the bag of potatoes, there are markers in the deep of God's provision. Paul talks about the secret of being content in Philippians 4, because he is confident in the fact that he and we,

"Can do all things through Him who gives me strength."
(Philippians 4:13)

He was steadfast in recognizing that God was his source. Paul was living out God's plan for his life and that was all that mattered. For you and me, we must:

Pray for Purpose,
Not Provision.
When you find your purpose,
You will then find provision.

Paul says with confidence to us,

"And my God will meet all your needs according to the riches of His glory, in Christ Jesus." (Philippians 4:19)

Remember, it's because of the markers that our faith and trust is developed, and we can know that God will not fail us.

Chapter Eight – A Bag of Potatoes

Chapter Nine
Platform

It was Oct. 30, 2001, 49 days after our nation had been attacked and our lives as Americans forever changed. The scene was Yankee stadium and game three of the World Series. The script couldn't have been written any better than to have the New York Yankees playing the Arizona Diamondbacks for the Major League Baseball championship. What happened was a piece of history which will be remembered for generations to come. George W. Bush, the 43rd President of the United States, was going to throw the first pitch to start the game, the first one played in the Bronx. It would be huge any year; this time, it was gargantuan. There was a statement to be made and it was not whether the President threw a strike or ball. In fact, it had nothing to do with baseball at all.

It was a rare moment when it didn't matter if you were a Republican or Democrat, or even a Yankees fan. We were all Americans and he was there to tell the world that we were not going to live in fear, nor were we going to stop being who we were. It was one of those moments that made us all proud to live in the United States of America.

President Bush was given a platform, and even though he was the leader of the free world, he was still human. It was impossible for his emotions to not take hold. He said, "I had never had such an adrenaline rush as when I finally made it to the mound. I was saying to the crowd, 'I'm with you, the country is with you...' and I wound up and fired the pitch. I've been to conventions and rallies and speeches: I've never felt anything so powerful and emotions so strong, and the collective will of the crowd so evident."

I think of other times, such as President Ronald Reagan standing at the Berlin Wall in 1987 and saying, "Mr. Gorbachev, open this gate, Mr. Gorbachev, tear down this wall!" Or Dr. Martin Luther King in 1963 calling for the end of racism. Before 250,000 people, he began his speech with the famous words, "I have a dream." These men were given significant platforms with the opportunity to make a statement and change the world.

Billy Graham used his platform to share the gospel with millions and countless lives were changed. There were others like D. L. Moody and George Whitfield, all with the gifting to speak to large crowds and impact the world. Mother Teresa was moved by the poverty and needs in India and used her platform as a Catholic nun to build the Missionaries of Charity. It grew to 600 missions, schools, and shelters in 120 countries.

A platform can be used for good or given to someone with an evil purpose and used to destroy lives. You think of dictators like Hitler, Mussolini, and in modern times, Sadaam Hussein. The 19 hijackers who crashed four planes into the World Trade Center, the Pentagon, and a field in

Pennsylvania were influenced by the platform of an evil man named Osama Bin Laden.

We were living in Waco in 1993, when David Koresh influenced a group of followers which led to the tragedy of the Branch Davidian compound and 82 lives lost. I could go on and on with examples like these of people who used their platforms to harm others.

A platform story you have not heard of happened in January 2012, and it is one I will never forget. It was in Northern Haiti near Cap-Haitien. I was with a group building a school in a remote village called Philibert. Each morning, we would load onto the back of a flatbed trailer and travel for two hours down country roads until we reached a field the driver would turn into. We would then travel through the fields for miles, passing other villages until we reached our destination.

I will never forget the children of Philibert; they lived in tiny huts and had a church and the school we were helping to build. The kids were happy, filled with joy, and incredibly appreciative of all they had.

On the 2nd day traveling to the village, we were caught in a roadblock that delayed us for several hours. It happened in front of a high school that was under construction.

Understand, in Haiti there is quite a variation of schools that children go to. They may meet under a tree, under a lean-to, or in some cases, there may be a building like in Philibert. I will never forget the images of children walking up the highways on their way to school with UNICEF uniforms, backpacks, and their heads held high. They believed their hope for a future was in receiving an education.

Unfortunately, due to politics, the high school had sat unfinished for several months. The students had grown frustrated, and what appeared to be an angry mob was actually teenagers determined to be heard. Until that happened, no one was going to move. When we got close enough to hear what they were saying, we heard, "If you don't open our school, we will die!" In the United States, it would probably seem overdramatic, but to these teens, they saw their future slipping away and this was their platform.

Sometimes there is a moment in time that distinguishes the opportunity for a platform. In reality, it is more than a moment or an event, it is a position or a place in life that may bring you to a moment.

Let's go back to the discovery of how God made each of us for a reason and how it will define our platform.

PREDESTINED

Paul writing in the book of Ephesians uses the word "predestined" to describe God's purpose for man. In chapter 1, he says,

"For He chose us in Him before the creation of the world to be holy and blameless in His sight. In love, He predestined us for adoption to sonship through Jesus Christ, in accordance with His pleasure and will." (v.4-6)

The NLT interpretation says, "God decided in advance," which blows away any theory of any of us being a mistake. The fact is, none of us throughout our lives, back to Adam and Eve, have been "holy and blameless."

So, it completed God's plan to send His Son to die for our sins and offer us redemption.

"In Him we have redemption through His blood, the forgiveness of sins, in accordance with the riches of God's grace that He lavished on us." (v.7-8)

Paul reiterates this point when he says,
"In Him we are also chosen, having been predestined according to the plan of Him who works out everything in conformity with the purpose of His will, in order that we, who were the first to put our hope in Christ, might be for the praise of His glory." (v.11-12)

Let's break this down. When we talk about finding God's purpose and plan for our lives, it is absolutely necessary that each of us understands that His only purpose is that we know Him and receive grace and redemption through His Son, Jesus Christ. Once that happens, then our life will evolve in the direction He has for us and His plan for us will be revealed.

If you jump over to 1 Timothy, Paul again makes it clear when he says that what pleases God is,

"[for] all people to be saved and to come to a knowledge of the truth."(v.2:4)

Typically, we begin in our high school years trying to determine what our career path will be, that will then lead to our occupation. Recently, I was looking over the bios of the graduating class of our local high school; 100% of the students listed a college they planned to attend. I couldn't help but wonder if any made decisions because they felt pressure so as not to be considered a failure.

The Washington Post ran a story that stated that only 27% of college graduates were working in a field that closely related to their major. To me, that is a staggering number.

After raising three teenagers and working with youth for many years, I believe it is incredibly important to not rush someone into a vocation. It is more important to direct them into a deep relationship with Jesus Christ so they can mature spiritually, which then will cause their emotional maturity. This will enable them to determine the plan God has for their lives.

This certainly can happen during the high school years or even before. My daughter, Amanda, knew from the time she was in first grade that she wanted to go to Texas A&M and pursue her education to be a teacher. She did, and just completed her fifth year of teaching 4th grade. It doesn't always happen like that and doesn't make anyone lesser or a failure.

If you hear what Paul is saying in Ephesians, then we must realize our purpose has nothing to do with vocation and everything to do with serving God.

**Purpose reveals God's Plan,
Plan creates our Platform.**

So, what pays the bills? Let's go to Romans 8, where it says,

"And we know that in all things God works for the good of those who love Him, who have been called according to His purpose." (v.28)

The Scripture sounds great, that we are to put God first and everything will work out. So, who puts food on the table and clothes on our backs? Herein lies our struggle as human beings. It's like I said in the last chapter about when faith seems to feel irresponsible. Where is the balance?

It totally goes against what society expects and requires. It comes down to the decision each of us make when we Go Deep under the surface of our lives and have the Word of God rooted and as the foundation of who we are. When we do, then we must believe and trust God and not worry. Yeah, I know, easy to say, not so easy to do.

Jesus was teaching about worry in Matthew 6 when He says,

"Therefore, I tell you, do not worry about your life, what you will eat or drink; or about your body, what you will wear. Is not life more than food, and the body more than clothes? Look at the birds of the air; they do not sow or reap or store away in barns, and yet your heavenly Father feeds them. Are you not much more valuable than they? Can any one of you by worrying add a single hour to your life? And why do you worry about clothes? See how the flowers of the field grow. They do not labor or spin. Yet I tell you that not even Solomon in all his splendor was dressed like one of these. If that is how God clothes the grass of the field, which is here today, and tomorrow is thrown into the fire, will He not much more clothe you-you of little faith?" (v.25-30)

The decision remains, do we believe the promises of the Bible? Jesus goes on and says,

"But seek first his kingdom and his righteousness and all these things will be given to you as well." (v.33)

The question again, how do we balance all this? This is where our platform comes into play. Know this: God doesn't fly by the seat of His pants. He carefully planned the universe, the earth, and mankind. He also planned each and every one of us and our lives were predestined. He knew when He formed us in our mother's womb there would be a place and an earthly reason for each of us, a platform.

He knew yours would be different than mine because the needs would be different. He gave us different gifts and abilities because He knew He would need to touch different people in different ways. Trust me, I have spent much of my adult life wishing I could sing like Michael W. Smith or act like Denzel Washington. I can't tell you how many times when my Dallas Cowboys needed a quarterback that I raised my hand and said, "God, I'm willing." Obviously, since I am writing this book, God didn't need me on the football field.

This I do know: God did need me for something else and He did give me a platform and the gifts and abilities to be used. He did the same for each of you. You may not see it, or you may feel like it has passed you by; don't believe it. Bring yourself to the place to know: He predestined you. When asked, Jesus said the greatest commandment is to, "love the Lord your God with all your heart and with all your soul and with all your mind and with all your strength." (Mark 12:30)

That's it, with everything you have. Then He said,

"The second is this: 'Love your neighbor as yourself.'"
(v.31)

Pretty simple, love God and then love your neighbor. You must love them enough to share your story of what Jesus has done for you. When you surrender to His purpose, which is to know Him, He will reveal His plan for your life and your platform will be given to you.

THE FISHERMEN

In Luke, we find the story of Jesus calling his first disciples. In the fourth chapter, He had overcome temptation from Satan and His ministry had kicked into high gear. Matthew refers to this as the time Jesus began to preach. Miracles happened wherever He went; one of those recorded is the healing of the mother-in-law of a man named Simon.

Chapter five of Luke takes Him to the shore of the lake of Gennesaret, where He was teaching. The more He taught, the bigger the crowds would become. He looked toward the water and saw two boats and fishermen, one being Simon, who were washing their nets. Jesus asked Simon to take Him out in the boat to continue teaching. Why do you think He did that?

Matthew 13 tells of a time when,

"Such large crowds gathered around Him that He got into a boat and sat in it, while all the people stood on the shore."(v.2)

It makes sense that He needed to create some distance in order to address the crowds. That could have been why that happened here, but I believe the reason goes even deeper because of what He did next.

When he finished speaking, He told Simon to,

"Put out into deep water and let down the nets for a catch." (Luke 5:4)

It wasn't because Jesus wanted to fish, He was testing their faith and obedience. The fishermen had been working all night and caught nothing, yet they did exactly what Jesus asked.

This wasn't Simon's first encounter with Jesus; he was a disciple of John the Baptist and had been previously introduced by his brother Andrew. The miracles, including in Simon's own family, were markers they could follow. This gave Simon and the others confidence they could do what Jesus told them to do, even when it didn't make sense.

The miracle happened, and the nets overflowed with fish, so much that the boats began to sink. Still, the purpose went deeper. His purpose was to show them that when they were obedient to what He told them to do, He would then provide for them beyond what they could imagine.

Obviously, the fish became unimportant because they left them behind at the end of the story.

Understand, Jesus was working with urgency. When you go back to chapter 4, you read that the people did not want Him to leave because He was working miracles. He said,

"...I must proclaim the good news of the kingdom of God to the other towns also, because that is why I was sent."
(v.43)

He was moved to touch as many as He could and fulfill His purpose. Let's go back to the original call in Luke 5 after the miracle of the full nets. Simon Peter and the others were blown away at what Jesus had just done. It was at this moment the lightbulb went off and they understood that this was the Son of God and they were not worthy of being in His presence. Jesus, said,

"Don't be afraid; from now on you will fish for people."(v.10)

The big picture of this story is about the fishermen. It was not only important to reach as many as He could, but His plan was also to raise up followers who would carry the message after He was gone. It's interesting, the first He chose were fishermen who had this unique ability and skill to catch fish, and a lot of them.

Fishing was their platform and God was going to use their abilities to continue to fish, but now, they lived for a bigger prize: the souls of people.

NAME CHANGE

There is something else significant about this story: the transition of Simon's name to Peter. You see him referred to as Simon in the beginning of the story and in verse 8, you see Simon Peter.

In similar fashion, when Saul of Tarsus, had a life-changing moment on the Road to Damascus, he was given a new identity and the name of Paul. Simon was a believer, yet he was about to have a new role and redefined platform.

As Jesus continued to perform miracles and teach, He also focused on developing the twelve who were His disciples. Like any good teacher, Jesus would teach and then test. One of those tests is found in Matthew 16, when He asked His disciples,

"Who do people say the Son of Man is?"(v.13)

They gave logical answers to great names of times past, which proved the lack of understanding of who He really was. Then He said,

"But what about you? Who do you say I am?"(v.14)

Simon Peter answered,

"You are the Messiah, the Son of the living God." (v.16)

He got it and was quickly becoming the leader of the band of men. Peter passed the test and the Lord was pleased and replied,

"Blessed are you, Simon son of Jonah, for this was not revealed to you by flesh and blood, but by My Father in heaven."

Then the change happened when He said,

"And I tell you that you are Peter, and on this rock, I will build My church, and the gates of Hades will not overcome it. I will give you the keys of the kingdom of heaven; whatever you bind on earth will be bound in heaven, and whatever you loose on earth will be loosed in heaven."(v.17-19)

This was a powerful statement and a transformational moment as Jesus prepared for His death and resurrection and was turning over the responsibility of building His kingdom to Peter.

He was saying this to an imperfect fisherman who He was now calling a rock. In just a few verses later, Jesus calls him Satan. We know of his impulsiveness, his denial, and his humiliation. We know who he became after the day of Pentecost: a courageous man who, until his own crucifixion, was greatly used and anointed to begin the church.

The transition of his name did not make him a different person with different skills and abilities. It meant that the skills and abilities God had given him were now to be used in a kingdom-building way.

Understand, he was still a fisherman, as was his brother Andrew, along with James and John. This was their platform. It's who they were and what they were good at. It was all part of God's plan when He predestined them.

There are many stories of men and women in the public eye and countless others we will never know who surrender their lives to Jesus and continue operating in their platform. They trained and were equipped to do what they do, now their focus and reason changes. They use their platform to glorify God and share their story of how they were redeemed by the blood of Jesus. This is Kingdom-building and how the church is built from the outside in. This is God's plan as to how the world will know of Him.

God is not calling you to be someone else. You have seen this message numerous times throughout this book. He is calling all of the redeemed to tell their stories and to use their platform.

It could be like Dante, sharing his story in his barbecue pit with men sitting around a table. It could be in a neighborhood or in a garage. It could be in an office tower or in a meeting room or a gym around workout equipment.

Part of the process of going deep, below the surface of our lives, is to discover all that God has for us and who He made us to be. It allows each of us to see God for who He truly is and how He views each of us.

The promised full life includes taking hold of your platform. It may lead to a moment in history that is heard around the world. More than likely, it will be a collection of many moments that happen in your everyday life that impact eternity.

Don't limit or deny who God made you to be, in the place and platform He has called you to. It will be an incredible ride that will last a lifetime and into eternity.

Chapter Ten
Seasons

In June of 1991, we were wrapping up a 10-day trip to Santiago, Chile. A group of 50, mostly teenagers, had been traveling across the country sharing music, drama, and testimonies in churches, schools, and theaters.

We had spent a portion of the week with professional soccer players who had found Christ. In popularity, they were the equivalent of NFL players in the United States. Every place we went there was mayhem when the athletes arrived. The word had traveled across the region about the Americans and the soccer players, and it had created quite a media frenzy. The players had a story, and they were using their platform to share it, and lives were being changed.

To say the least, it was an incredible experience that none of us will ever forget. Now, it was time to fly back to Texas and our regular routines. The day before our departure, the city was hit with a snowstorm followed by major flooding. We had traveled on the other side of the equator and the seasons were opposite. We were in the early days of winter. At home, the weather was sweltering near triple digits and to our families it was hard to imagine what was going on in Chile.

Santiago is a beautiful city which sits in a bowl, surrounded by the Andes Mountains. To fly out, pilots had to quickly gain altitude. It became a concern whether we would be able to take off due to the atmosphere and visibility. Fortunately, the weather cleared, and we were able to stay on schedule. I will never forget the trip nor this story.

To this day, I think of the power of the seasons and how they are different in various parts of the world and even in the United States. I spent many years traveling to Minnesota for business and quickly learned the impact winter has on that part of the country. To say it is cold doesn't do it justice. In Texas, we have the same extreme with the heat in the summer.

SPIRITUAL SEASONS

Just as the geographical seasons impact different parts of the country and the world, the seasons in our spiritual life do the same. By God's design there is contrast in each season and all are part of His sovereignty and in His control.

The beginnings of the message of Go Deep has been about God doing a work within us, a deep work. Now, with the added understanding of our platform, it's vital to know He does the work so He can equip us to reach others. This journey beneath the surface of our lives prepares us and creates the people God intends for us to be. It is not God's plan for His work to be exclusive, it is to be spread. As He develops us, He prepares us for each season of our lives and desires that each one will be productive and fruitful.

The Apostle Paul makes an interesting statement to his spiritual son, Timothy, when he says,

"...be prepared in season and out of season." (2 Tim. 4:2)

Paul knows his time is near and in the entire book of 2 Timothy you read the urgency in his words to his protege. He challenges him to not be timid and reminds him to fan into flame the gift of God which was on Timothy's life.

It's obvious that Paul recognizes human nature and the tendency to sink back. He is the coach near the end of the game, exhorting his star player to not let down. Paul is in prison for the final time and knows of the false teaching going on in the church. He tells stories of being deserted by people and reminds Timothy to stick to the gospel of Jesus Christ and to not get caught up in minutia. It gets really interesting when he speaks of terrible times and says,

"People will be lovers of themselves, lovers of money, boastful, proud, abusive, disobedient to their parents, ungrateful, unholy, without love, unforgiving, slanderous, without self-control, brutal, lovers of pleasure rather than lovers of God, having a form of godliness but denying its power." (2 Timothy 3:2-5)

You would think Paul was describing our society today. Maybe he was.

Timothy was a young pastor. That was his platform, but the principle of being prepared applies to any platform given by God. Paul had poured into his life and it was his responsibility to hold Timothy accountable to what he had learned. If not, he would get distracted and lose his focus on what really mattered. Just like you and I, Timothy was dealing with life and people and the changes the seasons bring. Paul continued to challenge him about the times and the urgency of the hour. He had to stay rooted in the message of the gospel, just like the bald cypress trees were rooted in the bottom of Reelfoot Lake.

Understand, Paul was in the last season of his life; he knew it and he could have shut down. He was alone and in prison, yet still his ministry and platform remained vibrant. The word 'difficult' doesn't do justice to the season he was in. Yet, he knew it was from God.

The lesson for us to understand is that all seasons are from God and are a part of His plan. No matter the season, we must not be distracted and be prepared for each opportunity it brings.

EMBRACE THE SEASONS

Two years before the trip to Chile, I started a new position as a Youth Minister. This was the first time I did not work bi-vocationally and was given the opportunity to commit all of my efforts toward ministry. When we arrived at the church, I met Craig. He was the only child of Jim and Ann and had grown up in this church.

Craig had graduated from high school the year before and was a gifted athlete, excelling on the baseball team. During his senior year after a minor car accident and broken collar bone, a cancerous tumor was found which led to major surgery.

When I met Craig, he was in the midst of radiation and preparing for chemotherapy. Honestly, my first impulse was to not get close, in fear of him dying. Just the opposite happened, and we formed a deep bond. His life was seemingly on hold and he would spend his days with me in my office. He became more like a younger brother than one of the youth. I loved him deeply and still do.

Craig wasn't a typical young man; he loved the Lord with everything in him and his maturity was well beyond his years. His commitment to Christ didn't happen when he got sick, it had been who he was from the time he was a little boy. He was the model son, close to both his mom and dad, and the guy every parent wanted their daughter to marry.

We had many deep conversations about his future. Never once did I sense the fear of death; he knew his life was in God's hands. He absolutely wanted to live, get married, have kids and a career. At the same time, he had a glimpse of heaven that literally gave him a peace that could not be understood.

This was a difficult season with surgeries and treatment, but it didn't stop him from living a full life. He was a leader amongst his peers and respected by all. It was not unusual to see him praying for people of all ages. He was the consummate encourager.

During his illness, we went on a mission trip to Mexico. He tirelessly walked the streets ministering to people and touching lives. At home, we had established a late-night hotline with one of the local rock stations. We would take calls from teenagers struggling with life. Craig was a regular working the phones, listening, encouraging, and praying for the callers.

We had hope that the surgery and treatment had taken care of the disease and celebrated when it was over. Unfortunately, it wasn't long until the cancer returned and spread throughout Craig's body. He died the way he lived, courageously and with his faith strong.

Craig left us in 1990 and as I write this, I still feel the emotion of his loss. Jim and Ann have remained close, not just as friends, but as family. Craig's impact on so many is still felt and the legacy he left at the age of 20 is remarkable.

The outcome was not what any of us wanted or understood. The question is still asked, "Why would God take the incredible only son of such wonderful people?" It's natural to wonder what Craig would have accomplished if he had lived. None of us have the answers to the questions.

Perhaps you have experienced a similar loss that, in the natural, makes no sense. Some believe it is wrong to ask God 'Why?' I don't. He is compassionate and cares. Psalm 34:18, says,

"The Lord is close to the brokenhearted and saves those who are crushed in spirit."

God doesn't ask us to understand, but He does ask us to trust. Personally, my time with Craig was as challenging a season as I can remember. It was heart-wrenching to let go of him and to know how much his parents were suffering. As difficult as it was, I am thankful I had the honor to be in Craig's life.

God's plan for me was different from others. I had the responsibility of helping teens grasp the death of someone so close to them, someone who was their leader and so young. To embrace the season in my life meant I had to rely more than ever on wisdom from God. I am thankful for His supernatural presence I felt during that time.

We talk about platform and stories. Craig's platform is his life and his death. Now it's up to me and others to share it, because someone needs to hear it. I only knew Craig during the time he was sick, and I had the opportunity to have a front-row seat as he embraced this difficult season. It certainly wasn't of his choosing, but he didn't allow it to stop him from taking hold of all God had for him. He was determined to make the most of each day.

There are seasons like this where our hearts are broken, and we wonder how we will go on. There are seasons in the valley and there are seasons on the mountaintop. There are seasons of rejoicing around weddings, births, and much more. There are seasons of favor when God's blessings are on everything we do, and seasons of challenge when we struggle for direction. Just as the author of Ecclesiastes wrote,

"There is a season for everything under the sun."
(Ecclesiastes 3:1]

We cannot control when the season comes nor what it contains. It could be influenced by something that happened or a decision. It all is part of God's plan and its timing is in His hands. A favorite Scripture for many is,

"And we know that in all things God works for the good of those who love Him, who have been called according to His purpose." (Romans 8:28)

To embrace the season, we must grab hold of this verse and the word 'ALL.' Paul didn't separate good things and bad things, it is the assurance that God is in ALL.

Even though we can't control the seasons in our lives, we do have the ability to do as Craig did and embrace whatever comes our way. He did so because as a young man, he had learned the value of what it meant to Go Deep and discovered all that God had for him.

LETTING GO

It's not hard to embrace a good season, but it's hard to let it go. As parents, we want to hang onto the years when our children are young, but we can't. That's not God's plan. On the other end of the spectrum, we do not want our parents to grow old, knowing the day will come when we have to say goodbye.

I confess, I am a hanger-on kind of guy. I struggle with letting go of things and people. I value solid friendships and believe they should last forever. My closest friends are ones I have had for decades.

It's important to understand that God brings people into our lives for seasons. I look back over the years and think of friends, still dear to me, yet our time together is over. God never fails to bring in new people for a different plan. Of course, this doesn't relate to spouses and family, we are cemented together for life.

Remember when you were a kid and your parents would tell you when it was time to be home or come inside? Did you ever use the phrase "But Mom, But Dad!"? You would go into some lame excuse as to why whatever you were doing was too important to stop. Even as adults, sometimes we overvalue our importance, and when God closes a door, we resist and try to keep it open. Am I the only one who has argued with God about how I couldn't stop because I wasn't finished? The problem is, the conversation always revolved around "I." Letting go of a season means to trust God's plan and to know it's bigger than you or I. Isaiah 43:18 says,

"Forget the former things; do not dwell on the past."

This is a powerful passage which actually began in verse 16, when the Lord is reminding us who He is and who has made the way for all of us. The other reason to let go follows in verse 19,

"See I am doing a new thing! Now it springs up; do you not perceive it?"

Why do you think God is asking us if we perceive it? Could it be because we have lost focus on who He is and what He has done, and we are not letting go?

I love the change of seasons, some more than others. My favorite is when the winter ends and the Texas bluebonnets begin to bloom, and the dormant grass becomes green again. I love it because it also signals baseball is on the horizon.

Crazy as it sounds, I enjoy the heat of the Texas summer with longer days and beautiful sunrise and sunsets. I love the fall with different colors and the beginning of football season, holidays, and family. Then there is the beauty of the snow when it covers the ground during the winter.

We cannot enjoy a new season until we let go of the one we are in. After a hard season, we are anxious for change, but even after a productive season, we must know there is a "new thing" waiting on the horizon.

LEARN FROM THE SEASONS

In the business world, I maintained a principal when leading teams. After every event that happened or when an incident occurred, we would ask ourselves the question, "What did we learn?" It didn't matter whether it was a positive situation or negative, there was always something we could learn in order to be better. In most cases, we would discover things we would have done differently if we had the chance for a do-over.

God doesn't give us do-overs, but He does give us next chances. The things we learn in all seasons of life will help us accomplish all He has for us, if we allow it to.

Go Deep is permeated on the premise of being better. It doesn't necessarily mean we are bad, it just means we aren't satisfied and want to be the best we can be. We believe there is more. It is a process that should never stop, and the most valuable lessons learned are from our experiences in the different seasons of our lives.

We learn by asking God - It may be in the midst of the season or after a season is over when you open your heart in prayer and say, God what are you wanting to teach me? David prayed in Psalm 25:4,

"Show me Your ways, Lord, teach me Your paths."

There is the old adage that says, "You are never too old to learn," which is true. It's the same, no matter how long we have served God, we must never stop learning and growing.

We learn through God's Word - I have found this so true in writing this book. This has been a special season for me to step out in faith. Countless times, the Scriptures have been illuminated for me and I have grasped something for the first time. Another great Psalm says,

"I will instruct you and teach you in the way you should go." (32:8)

We can only learn if we are teachable and open. Learning through the seasons means to align all that we have accomplished or lost with God's Word.

We learn through wise counsel - God places people in our lives who are sincere in their desire to help us grow and learn. We should value wisdom from those whose life demonstrates a strong relationship with Christ. Their purpose is heartfelt and there is not an agenda outside of being a support. We live in a day where trust is easily compromised, and many are less willing to take the risk to allow someone to speak into their lives. We can go back to the example the Apostle Paul gives us in 2 Timothy when he spoke into Timothy's life. He had nothing to gain and much to lose, yet his love for Timothy compelled him. He spoke into the seasons of life that Timothy was experiencing and gave wisdom and insight to help him grow and be productive.

RESPOND TO THE SEASONS

As Paul winds down his challenge to Timothy and tells him to

"be prepared in season and out of season"

He gets more specific about what he is to do and the difficulty it will bring. He says to,

"correct, rebuke and encourage - with great patience and careful instruction." (2 Timothy 4:2)

He goes on to talk about the times he will face with people. Timothy must be prepared to deal with more compromised teaching that will be accepted and desired. He had work to do and Paul's instruction was to,

"keep your head in all situations, endure hardship, do the work of an evangelist, discharge all the duties of your ministry." (v.5)

The urgency of the hour remains, and the words Paul spoke to Timothy are for us today. The division in our culture is at a critical level. It is felt in politics, the business world, sports, churches, and even in families. As a society we respond reactively to the latest crisis that adds to the division. It is a time like never before that God's people should be the voice of calm and healing. Instead, some are joining in the rancor or sitting on the sidelines. We have seemingly become distracted by either the devastation or the euphoria of the seasons.

I don't know what impact the seasons of your life have had on where you are today. It is my hope and my prayer that the message of Go Deep has motivated you to be better and to recognize there is more that God has for each of us. It is through the different seasons, good and bad, that God will mold us to be more like Christ and use the experiences to equip us to be all that He has made us to be.

Maybe you are feeling the effects of a difficult season or seasons in your life and it is keeping you from moving forward. I get it, we have all been there. It's then we can take hold of the words of Jesus when He said,

"Come to Me, all you who are weary and burdened, and I will give you rest. Take My yoke upon you and learn from Me, for I am gentle and humble in heart, and you will find rest for your souls." (Matthew 11: 28-29)

My friends, the seasons of our lives will make us or break us. When you Go Deep, you will discover the "rest" Jesus promised. With it, you will find healing, a full life, and the person He made you to be.

"There is a time for everything and a season for every
activity under the heavens:

a time to be born and a time to die,
a time to plant and a time to uproot,
a time to kill and a time heal,
a time to tear down and a time to build,
a time to weep and a time to laugh,
a time to mourn and a time to dance,
a time to scatter stones and a time to gather them,
a time to embrace and a time to refrain from embracing,
a time to search and a time to give up,
a time to keep and a time throw away,
a time to tear and a time to mend,
a time to be silent and a time to speak,
a time to love and a time to hate,
a time for war and a time for peace."
Ecclesiastes 3:1-8

Chapter Eleven
A Movement

In the beginning of the book, I referred to Go Deep as the launch of a movement. To be honest, I hesitated with that description due to the fact that we are a society filled with movements and typically they run for a season and go away. In many cases, they are in response to an event or situation, and a group of people want a platform to express their displeasure.

Movements have an impact when people come together with shared passion and a commitment to a certain cause. It is not uncommon for large movements to form a march or protest in order to gain visibility. Many times, they get attention until a new event happens and takes center stage.

With the advent of social media, there is an additional powerful resource. It gives the ability to spread a message in more places than ever, typically, with a hashtag such as #godeepmovement. It has allowed a forum for action without people being physically present.

During my lifetime, there have been many different kinds of movements, some I align with and some that I don't. Personally, I am not one to march or hold signs. I'm not saying it's wrong, it just doesn't fit the way I operate, and I am not sure of the long-term benefit.

This last chapter will tie together all the pieces of what we have discovered in our quest to Go Deep. The book began with the individual work that God must do in each of us, independent of anyone else. The personal process must happen, then it is God's plan to pull us together in agreement. Once we come together, the question is, what do we do now?

A MOVEMENT TO MODEL

Movements didn't start in our lifetime; they date back to both the Old and New Testament. The book of Acts details the story of perhaps the greatest movement in history. It started with 120 people whose lives had been completely upended after three unbelievable years of following Jesus. They had been given hope, had it taken away, supernaturally given back and then gone again. There is nothing that happened that Jesus had not prepared them for. Still it was beyond comprehension.

Acts begins with Jesus still on the scene. After His resurrection, He spent another 40 days teaching and preparing His disciples for what was about to happen. They had just witnessed the most unbelievable story ever told. His plan was for them to take the story to the ends of the earth.

The power of what began in this movement, which we call the Early Church, didn't last for just a season. It was more than a response to the events they had witnessed, it was based on life change, and it was only just beginning.

FAITH COMMUNITY

In our society, you say the word Church, and most will think of a building, location, or sometimes a well-known pastor. There are buildings of all shapes and sizes, traditional and modern, and in some countries, even underground. Churches rent schools, storefronts, rodeo arenas, and meet under tents.

The latest trend of large churches is to have multiple campuses with the leader projected on a big screen. We attended a local megachurch where the main Pastor was literally in 3D and looked incredibly present. The only difference was he was about 10 feet tall. As I shared earlier, technology can be a wonderful thing and allows the church to connect in ways like never before. How many lives were impacted when Billy Graham hit the television screen with the message of salvation?

Still, today's church is a far cry from the original group of 120. They started in an upper room which has been described to me as a place that was like a large family room. It's important that we get past a place and recognize that the Church is not a building of any kind. It is made up of God's people, and the model was established in this story in Acts.

It's not necessarily a bad thing that through the years the church has become "organized" unless the organization takes precedence over God's purpose. We only need to look at the early church and ask ourselves if we still operate by the same Biblical standards.

They were all in - They had experienced miracles and the death and resurrection. When Jesus commanded them to go to Jerusalem and wait, they did. He was gone, and they could have gone back to their former lives. I am sure there was natural uncertainty; still, there was no turning back. Isn't this what an experience with Jesus should do to all of us? Because of their commitment and obedience, the movement began.

They plugged into the power source - Jesus said to His disciples,

"But you will receive power when the Holy Spirit comes on you; and you will be My witnesses in Jerusalem, and in all Judea and Samaria, and to the ends of the earth." (Acts 1:8)

He was leaving, but not leaving them alone. The Holy Spirit, the third person of the Trinity, was coming. Notice the words, "on you," the Holy Spirit's purpose is to take over. When the Holy Spirit did come, in Acts 2, it says they were "filled" (v.4). Even though there would no longer be the humanity of Jesus, the same presence was on them, filling them.

Go back to John 14, when Jesus was preparing the disciples and says,

"If you love Me, keep My commands, and I will ask the Father, and He will give you another advocate to help you and be with you forever - the Spirit of truth. The world cannot accept Him, because it neither sees Him nor knows Him. But you know Him, for He lives with you and will be in you." (v.15-17)

The definition of the word advocate is, "one who pleads the cause of another." Other Bible translations use comforter or helper. This word is significant because it implies that the work is now ours and God will supply the power and support, we need to get it done.

There is great debate in the church world about this section of the Bible and its interpretation. Some embrace it, some deny it, some ignore it, and some believe it was only for the original Apostles. I choose to embrace it. In my simple way of thinking, I can't grasp why God would not empower us today. The world we live in desperately needs to hear the same message they heard in Acts, and we need the same power given to the early believers.

This movement began when changed men boldly proclaimed the message of Jesus and lives were changed.

They learned and prayed together - The Scriptures say,

"They devoted themselves to the apostles teaching, the breaking of bread and to prayer." (Acts 2:42)

Picture this movement of people who were hungry to grow and know more. I can see them crowding around the apostles, who as disciples, had sat under the teaching of Jesus. They told of the Old Testament forefathers, the miracles Jesus had performed and His death and resurrection. Because of this, each day people were saved (v.47).

Can you imagine hearing them tell the stories of Jesus turning water into wine and when He fed 5000 with five loaves of bread and two fish? Can you hear the emotion in their voices when they share the story of Jesus calming the storm? How about when they told about the raising of Lazarus? I bet there was grief and tears when they spoke of the betrayal of Judas.

Oh, then there was Peter. Listen as he tells the ups and downs of his relationship with Jesus. I am sure he talked about when he walked on water and when he cut off the ear of the servant. I wonder if he was overcome with emotion and perhaps even fell to his knees with remorse when he told of his denial.

This wasn't your typical Bible study where you can choose your favorite translation, because there wasn't any! This was the New Testament being written! We know, that when the apostles spoke, lives were changed.

They did life together - It started with 120 and after the day of Pentecost, Peter, filled with the power of the Holy Spirit, spoke, and the movement grew, adding 3000 (2:41). Imagine that, a 2400% increase, without church growth programs, any new buildings, social media, or any kind of marketing. It was the power of God changing lives by the Holy Spirit through His people.

All of a sudden, this movement was moving with jet fuel, and there were needs among the new believers. They were mesmerized by the

"many signs and wonders performed by the apostles."
(v.43)

The bigger the group, the more needs there were. They didn't turn to the government; they took care of each other. They ate together and prayed together (v.42). Chapter 4 talks about how they, "Were one in heart and mind" (v.32) and they didn't even consider their possessions as their own. This was radical and today would be considered cultish. These believers realized what they had seen and experienced was of eternal value and earthly possessions didn't compare.

It was more than the physical act of being together; it was a heart issue. There is a powerful story told in Mark 10. A man sees Jesus and runs up to Him and falls on his knees. This man is wealthy, yet in his heart he knows there is more and is concerned about his eternal destiny, so he asked,

"What must I do to inherit eternal life?" (Mark 10:17)

Jesus takes him to the commandments of the "things" he should and should not do. This was a test because Jesus already knew his heart. The man knew he was keeping the commandments, but there was still uncertainty, rightfully so. It's those times when on the outside you are living the right life, but there is still a lack of peace because of what is on the inside.

The next part of this story is even more compelling, it says,

"Jesus looked at him and loved him." (v.21)

Stop there for a moment and grab hold of those words. Jesus knew what was in his heart. He didn't beat him over the head with a club, He loved him and then spoke truth to him and said,

"One thing you lack, Go, sell everything you have and give to the poor, and you will have treasure in heaven. Then come, follow Me." (v.21)

Jesus spoke directly into his heart because He knew exactly what was keeping the man from the peace he was searching for. Perhaps he had inherited his wealth, or maybe he had built his business, we don't know. Either way, it owned his heart and was keeping him from the full life offered by Jesus. The Bible says,

"At this, the man's face fell. He went away sad because he had great wealth." (v.22)

It is about a willingness and obedience to truly put our relationship with Christ above the things we own. My friends, this story applies to today's faith community. So many struggle with just giving back to God the small portion He asks. In reality, for a true believer, all we have should be His. This was the mindset of the early movement. Following Jesus was all that mattered and all they had belonged to Him. The same must apply to a movement of people who truly desire to Go Deep, to be willing to lay aside the surface things of this life in return for having the full life promised by Jesus.

GO DEEP AND PRAY

I believe when it says they prayed together, it was in response to what was being said. Obviously, they prayed prayers of repentance and surrender because their numbers grew. I am sure they prayed for their loved ones who had not heard the message and they prayed for each other.

Have you ever listened to someone share their story under such an anointing, it makes you want to fall to your knees and pray? It's important that we grasp this; it is the Spirit of God who draws people. Anything else is surface and artificial. These men had an encounter with God that changed them, and because the spirit of God was ON them, people were drawn to them.

The core Scripture of the Go Deep movement is,

"Let the redeemed of the Lord tell their story - those He redeemed from the hand of the foe." (Psalm 107:2)

This is our calling, to tell our stories of what Jesus has done in our lives. We do it by the power of the Holy Spirit on us. I believe with everything in me that when we do, lives will be changed, and people will cry out to the Lord and He will rescue them.

GO DEEP IN GOD'S WORD

I recently sat in a home group, and the discussion was about sharing our faith. One person mentioned how they didn't feel knowledgeable enough about the Bible to be comfortable sharing with someone else. This is a common struggle of many faithful Christians. This person has a wonderful story of what God has done for their family. It is a story that would touch the heart of anyone who hears it.

I am thankful for wise, educated theologians who instruct us and give insight into God's Word. It is critical for every believer to study the Word of God because it is a lamp and a light, meant to give us direction. I have found when I Go Deep to discover all that God has for me, then it creates a hunger for more of Him, which means more of His Word. It no longer feels like a duty and becomes a passion.

Friends, with that understanding, study God's Word while never negating the power of your story; there are people today who need to hear it. Like mine, it may not be the storyline you see in movies. Whatever path your life has followed, it is a story of the mercy and grace of a loving Savior, that's all that matters.

OPPOSITION

For every movement established, there is resistance and opposition. When there is a Pro-this, then there is always a Pro-that. It's always interesting that there is equal passion and belief on both sides of whatever the cause.

This was no different for the early church. The same religious leaders who called for the crucifixion of Jesus were now opposing the movement. They threw Peter and John in jail, yet they still couldn't stop the momentum as now the number of believers had grown to 5000. I love what Acts 4:13 says,

"When they saw the courage of Peter and John and realized they were unschooled, ordinary men, they were astonished, and they took note that these men had been with Jesus."

Stop and reread those words and let them sink in. Remember, these were the same fishermen whom Jesus had called. They were the ones who had feared the wind and the waves.

If it were today, some might say they didn't have the credentials or education needed to do what they were doing. What they had was all they needed; they had been with Jesus. It wasn't about the style of the clothes they wore, the amount of money they had in the bank, the position they held, their denomination or their education. None of these are wrong, but they are not what brings the power of God on our lives, they are surface things.

Just as He did then, He does today; He chooses ordinary people to empower. It's the same brokenness, humility, and surrender that God looks for when He releases His anointing. The anointing was necessary because God knew there would be opposition to the movement, and He knew there would be opposition today.

It was the same when the Lord said to Joshua to be strong and courageous repeatedly as he took the mantle from Moses. The battle was more than the 40 years in the desert. In fact, after they crossed the Jordan River, in many ways, the battle had just begun. Under Moses' leadership, they defeated two Kingdoms. Under Joshua, 31 kingdoms had to be conquered. They arrived at their destiny but still had to possess it.

The same is true of our spiritual destiny: we must take it. The opposition is not people, or flesh and blood as referenced in Ephesian 6:12. It's bigger than that; it is a spiritual battle that Paul called "authorities, powers of this dark world and spiritual forces of evil." The good news is, we have available to us all that we need to overcome the enemy. (Ephesians 6:13-17) We must be filled with the courage of Joshua and the Apostles while we put on the full armor that Paul teaches us.

He is clear when he uses the words "put on" that they are actions we must take. He uses the word "stand" three times in two verses, the last time adding the word firm. You are able to stand firm because the armor gives you the protection and the weapons you need.

When we are completely surrendered to our faith in Jesus, we wear the belt of truth, meaning we are kept together, and we buckle it around us. The breastplate of righteousness protects our heart, which is the center of who we are and where everything flows through. It's then we are ready because we are "fitted with the gospel of peace." It's the peace that Jesus promised us in John 14:27. Even more protection comes with the shield of faith, the "confidence in what we hope for and assurance about what we do not see." (Hebrews 11:1) It gets better and stronger when we put on the helmet of salvation. Grasp the power of that, the blood of Jesus covering our minds and capturing our thoughts. Finally, we take up the Word of God, which Paul calls the sword of the Spirit. It is offensive and gives us the weapon we need to conquer. You add on the next verse where Paul says to pray, not just every once in a while, but "on all occasions." These are the steps we do individually and independently. The armor and prayer provide us with everything we need to be successful in a spiritual battle. (Ephesians 6:10-18)

Understand, it's not a political or social battle. So often we make people or a group our enemy. I am not a "devil in every corner" guy. With that said, we must not be spiritually naïve and realize we as a country and society have turned our back to the things of God. For so long, Americans have been a beacon not only of freedom, but of faith in God Almighty. Those were the values our country was built upon and today are continuously under attack for the sake of diversity.

The lessons we have learned from the Children of Israel must not be overlooked. The most consistent thing about God's chosen people was their inconsistency. When times would get tough, how quickly they would turn to other gods. The book of Joshua tells of the conquests and the division of the land they had been promised. You would think after all God had done for them, they would not waver from serving only Him. Then there is the book of Judges.

The generation of Joshua had experienced so many great things that the Lord had done for Israel. You would think the legacy left would be strong, and the next generation would continue to serve God, but no. Unbelievably, in chapter 2, we read these words, "they knew neither the Lord nor what He had done for Israel." How does that happen? These were God's chosen people who He had delivered from the hands of the Egyptians and ultimately gave them the Promised land. Think of all the stories and miracles that had happened. I find it inconceivable that they couldn't have known. Yet the Bible says,

"The Israelites did evil in the eyes of the Lord and served Baals. They forsook the Lord, the God of their ancestors, who had brought them out of Egypt." (Judges 2:11-12)

It's tragic because it is not the only time we see the words "evil in the eyes of the Lord." You even see the word "again" as God's chosen people continued to have utter disregard of the things of God. Sound familiar? Do you see the same in today's society? Somehow there are many who do not know God, nor what He has done. I ask myself, do my grandchildren know the story of the bag of potatoes and the miracles He has done for my family, generation after generation? I want them to tell of what Jesus has done for us so they, too, will understand and believe and experience the power of Almighty God. What about you? Is the legacy you are building filled with markers for your children and grandchildren to see?

WHAT REALLY MATTERS

Throughout the book, you have seen the reference to "surface things." What do these words really mean? When you Go Deep, you separate the things that have eternal value with the things that are temporary, the surface things.

We are so blessed in the United States with the biggest and the best. When the latest iPhone is released, we wait for hours outside the Apple store to get the latest and greatest. It's interesting, the next year, what we waited for is obsolete, and we are back in line again. The list of things that are "must haves" is long. I don't believe it is necessarily wrong to possess things, unless those things become what we live for. Think back to the story of the rich young ruler where those things hindered him from experiencing what had eternal value. (Mark 10:17-31)

I think often of the children in the village of Philibert, Haiti. They live in tiny huts and have a school and a church. I was told they celebrate Christmas by sharing a can of Coke. To some of us, this would seem devastating and hopeless, yet these kids are filled with more joy than I have ever experienced. In my mind's eye, I will always remember their smiles and their welcome when they stood in front of their church and sang to us songs about Jesus. We leave our comfort zones and head to these remote places with great hopes of being a blessing. What I have found each time, I am the one who is changed and blessed.

My thoughts then come to our culture and society. Just in the last few months, we hear of well-known people, even Pastors, who could not find the hope the children of Philibert had in Christ and took their own lives. In surface living, it is hard to comprehend people who supposedly have everything but cannot find a reason to live. I understand, there are so many complexities around mental illnesses that drive people to a hopeless point. I am thankful I have never gotten to that point, even in my darkest moments. It is on us, as Christians, to not look to the earthly successes and assume someone has it all. I do know and believe that God's purpose is for all to have life to the full as I have mentioned over and over throughout the chapters of this book. Without Christ, I can understand why someone would feel hopeless, even if they had everything this world has to offer. No matter how much we gain here on earth, there will never be enough to satisfy our souls.

For believers in the movement, we must pray for one another like never before. My heart goes out to Pastors and leaders of the faith community. The attack on what we believe in our generation has never been stronger. Because of this, it is critical that we do not look to the surface things to reach people. We must remain steadfast to the purity and power of God's Word and leading people into a life-changing experience with Jesus. The death and resurrection of Jesus brought hope to the movement in Acts, and it will bring hope to us today.

To Go Deep with God will allow Him to separate for you the things of eternal value and the surface things. Open your heart and allow the Holy Spirit to reveal to you what matters most to Him. When you do, then you will truly understand when 1 Peter 1:8 speaks to the "inexpressible and glorious joy" that comes from knowing Jesus.

THERE IS MORE

Imagine with me, a movement of people who live their life with a passion for more. To these people, the surface things of life would become less important than finding out what lies beneath the surface. They would be completely committed to be all that God created them to be, no matter the cost. I believe these people would change our world.

As you have read, it begins with each of us individually allowing the excavator to dig beneath the surface of our lives. It is then, through the work of the Holy Spirit, that any garbage that hinders us can be removed, no matter how long it's existed or how big it is. When this happens, we will surely find God's "wonderful deeds in the deep" and the full life Jesus promised.

The Go Deep movement doesn't have a rule book of what it looks like. It can be men meeting in a barbecue restaurant telling their stories as they help each other be better. It can be a group of young couples meeting together on a back porch, supporting each other to raise their families to be all that God created them to be. How about a group of students coming together with their peers with honest, open, and transparent conversation that helps them deal with their fears? Can you imagine with me, a group of people in corporate America meeting in a break room or even a board room? I can see farmers meeting over breakfast in a local diner. I see athletes who have spent their lives training to reach their goals, humbling themselves and finding hope for their souls. I could go on and on. It's not complicated; in fact, it's pretty simple.

If you are a football fan, the title of this book may have gotten your attention. As kids, in our front yards or maybe out in a field, we would get in a huddle. The quarterback would look at the receivers and say GO DEEP. It meant when the ball was hiked to run your hardest and fastest. He would rear back and throw the ball as far as he could, hoping his receiver was there to catch it for a touchdown. Sometimes, it was a last-ditch effort to win the game. It was all or nothing. I don't know about you, but as a Christian who wants more, to Go Deep motivates me to run as fast as I can toward the end zone to change the game and ultimately win.

Paul writing to Timothy said,

"I have fought the good fight, I have finished the race, I have kept the faith." (2 Timothy 4:7)

Who are you thinking about in your world that wants more and will Go Deep as a believer? Who in your life is without Christ that would welcome a loving, non-judgmental conversation to help them be better? You might be surprised, I know I was when my next-door neighbor showed up at Go Deep in Dante's restaurant.

Will you join the movement? It simply means you will tell Jesus that you want more of Him. You want all He has for you, and you will do whatever He wants in order to receive it. God has given each of us a platform, all different, yet waiting to be used for His purpose. He has also given each of us a story, a story that someone is waiting to hear and only you can tell it.

GO DEEP

GO DEEP

ABOUT THE AUTHOR

David Bryant is a businessman and communicator. He is the founder and President of RSM Communications LLC, a solutions company specializing in training and consulting. Over the past 40 years, he has had a diverse career working in ministry, local small business and corporate America. David is passionate about marketplace ministry and equipping business owners to use their platforms to impact the Kingdom of God.

David is a native Texan who grew up in Dallas. He and his wife of 39 years, LeeAnne, reside in Celina, north of the DFW metroplex and are blessed with 3 outstanding adult children, their spouses, and 4 perfect grandchildren.

You can schedule David to speak at your church or for your organization by contacting him at dbryant@rsmcommunications.net

GO DEEP

GO DEEP

GO DEEP

GO DEEP

Disclaimer & Copyright Information

GO DEEP

GO DEEP

GO DEEP

GO DEEP

CPSIA information can be obtained
at www.ICGtesting.com
Printed in the USA
LVHW111641160621
690388LV00007B/17